Bible Readings FOR CAREGIVERS

In honor of my mother,
Amy Halvorson Groth,
whose life was filled
with care for others.
With love and gratitude.

Bible Readings

FOR
CAREGIVERS

•

Betty Groth Syverson

AUGSBURG Publishing House • Minneapolis

Scripture quotations unless otherwise noted are from the Holy Bible: New International Version. Copyright 1978 by the New York International Bible Society. Used by permission of Zondervan Bible Publishers.

Library of Congress Cataloging-in-Publication Data

Syverson, Betty Groth, 1926–
    Bible readings for caregivers.
      1. Nurses—Prayer-books and devotions—English.
2. Nurses' aides—Prayer-books and devotion—English.
I. Title.
BV4596.N8S96   1987   242'.68   87-17540
ISBN 0-8066-2276-8

Manufactured in the U.S.A.   APH 10-0695

PREFACE

We all have opportunities to show caring to others in our daily lives. Caregiving is not limited to the professionals. Whenever we reach out in empathy to someone in need we are caregivers. We may stand beside a mourner at a graveside, comfort the ill, or bring cheer to a lonely person. We may allow a person to express feelings about a job loss or the agony of a divorce. As a member of the body of Christ, "if one part suffers, every part suffers with it" (1 Cor. 12:26). If we listen through the pain, walk with the person through troubled times, and present a word of hope in Christ, we offer Christian caring.

Through nursing we often touch people at crossroads moments of their lives. Something has happened which may alter their path in living, in work, or in outlook.

In this book many truths of God's Word are applied to varied experiences, largely medically related. Many are my own; many are those of others.

Of great inspiration to me are the elderly from whom I have learned about tolerance, gentleness, patience, and a rock-like faith which allows them to view their passing from this life as fulfillment of a promise for their eternal home.

"Look to the Lord and his strength; seek his face always" (Ps. 105:4).

"Whatever you do, work at it with all your heart, as working for the Lord, not for men. . . . It is the Lord Christ you are serving" (Col. 3:23-24).

Lord,
make me an instrument of Your peace.
Where there is hatred let me sow love;
where there is injury, pardon;
where there is doubt, faith;
where there is despair, hope;
where there is darkness, light;
and where there is sadness, joy.

O Divine Master,
grant that I may not so much seek
   to be consoled, as to console;
to be understood as to understand;
to be loved as to love.
For it is in giving that we receive;
it is in pardoning that we are pardoned;
and it is in dying that we are born
   to eternal life.

Attributed to St. Francis of Assisi
(c. 1181-1226)

■ A PSALM FOR CAREGIVERS

Psalm 148: "Let them praise the name of the Lord, for his name alone is exalted; his splendor is above the earth and the heavens" (v. 13).

As you read this psalm in its entirety, picture yourself at the base of the majestic Teton mountains with antiphonal choirs singing this song of praise, full and intense, in blending harmonies.

The awesome beauties of nature have stirred many a heart. Do you ever feel this sense of praise at the beginning of your day? It is easy to feel the burden of work, but how good if we can start by praising God.

Praise the Lord.
Praise him for his healing powers for heart, and mind and soul.
Praise him for doctors, dedicated to serving you.
Praise him for nurses committed to excellence in care.
Praise him for nursing assistants who speak with love, who touch with gentleness and patience.
Praise him for all who serve in their goal toward good health.
Praise the Lord for chaplains
who bear soul-cares and ease hearts concerns.
Praise him for social workers who smooth the paths for recovering patients, who direct them to helping hands.

 For those who touch another's life with your love, we praise and thank you, Lord.

Identify other psalms of praise in your Bible.

■ SET ASIDE A SHALOM PLACE

Rev. 3:20: "Here I am! I stand at the door and knock. If anyone hears my voice and opens the door, I will come in and eat with him, and he with me."

Today problems of the entire world permeate homes or cars at the flick of a switch. More than ever we need a place for quiet, for meditation, for prayer. A shalom place, a center of peace.

"Be still and know that I am God" (Ps. 46:10). We need aloneness to be effective in our togetherness. We know the importance of proper food, rest, and exercise. Equally as vital to Christian caregivers is the nourishment of our souls by studying God's word and spending time in prayer each day. "Grow in the grace and knowledge of our Lord Jesus Christ" (2 Peter 3:18).

Christ stands at our heart's door, knocking. We must invite him in to "sup" with us. As with family we open the door for him, and present our own needs and our concerns for others.

As we sit quietly in God's presence, we ponder our many blessings, "always giving thanks to God the Father for everything, in the name of our Lord Jesus Christ" (Eph. 5:20). Our hearts overflow in gratitude and praise. "Through Jesus, therefore, let us continually offer to God a sacrifice of praise" (Heb. 13:15).

 Thank you, Lord, that we can pour out our hearts to you, as a child to a parent.

Do you have a shalom place?

10

■ FEARFULLY AND WONDERFULLY MADE

Ps. 139:14-16: "I praise you, because I am fearfully and wonderfully made; your works are wonderful, I know that full well" (v. 14).

I remember my deep sense of awe when I learned how our body fights infection, how alternate circulatory routes become established when one vessel is obstructed, and how a network of nerves forms an early warning system to signal potential problems.

"How could any doctor not believe in God?" I wondered.

Our bodies are a collection of miracles. We have a brain which sends out messages at 250 miles per hour, acting like a superb computer. Our heart, as a lifeline pump, sends blood through 75,000 miles of vessels 100,000 times a day. As pollution control centers, our lungs constantly convert bad air to good air. Like the finest chemical plant, our digestive system converts meat and potatoes into the energy of life. Light converts to vision, vibrations to sound, and 60 trillion separate cells function harmoniously.

Can we take a single breath for granted? Of course we do, yet if we ponder these miracles, we know our body is a collection of marvelous functions. Its capabilities seem boundless. We are indeed fearfully and wonderfully made.

 We praise you, Lord, for our extraordinary bodies and for the potentials of our minds. Grant us, Lord, a heart of compassion that we may serve you by serving those in need.

Write a psalm of praise for the gift of life.

■ ROLE MODEL FOR CAREGIVERS

Luke 10:25-37: "Love the Lord your God with all your heart and with all your soul and with all your strength and with all your mind, and 'Love your neighbor as yourself.' " (v. 27).

Here we see the triangle of strength needed for caregivers. First, our whole-hearted love for God, then reaching out to others with that love. But the assumed baseline is revealed in the last two words, "as yourself." If we don't love ourselves, how can we reach out to help others?

In this familiar story we see the good Samaritan, a man looked down upon by Jews, feeling compassion toward a man who had fallen into the hands of robbers. He helped the injured man by binding up his wounds, and medically served him by pouring oil and wine into the affected areas. He shared his own possessions with him by putting the man on his own donkey. He spent the time needed to transport the victim to an inn and paid for his keep. Then he solicited the innkeeper's support by asking him to "Look after him," he said, "and when I return I will reimburse you for any extra expense you may have" (v. 35).

Our caregiving may be as complete as the good Samaritan's or we may simply be a physical presence at the side of a hurting person.

 Thank you for the model of caregiving, Lord, in the example of the good Samaritan and in the work of caring people whose lives have been a blessing to us.

Let us remember that care can not be given unless it is willingly received.

◼ LOVE REMEMBERED

John 15:12-17: "My command is this: Love each other as I have loved you" (v. 12).

In my haste to complete the weekly blood pressure checks at our nursing home, I barely knocked as I pushed open the door of her room.

"Martha,—I, ah—"

With uncommonly moist eyes, she looked up from her open letter. She smiled as I hesitated. Was I interrupting a very private moment? "That's all right," she said. Her frail left hand caressed a stack of letters. Shakily, she folded the open page.

"I have to dispose of my trunkful of momentos," she explained. "Our house was sold. I was just reading letters from my husband for the last time. He wrote these just before we were married."

A pink flush lightened her finely etched face as she added, "I had forgotten how much I meant to him."

I was deeply touched to know that the same warmth and love which her husband had communicated to her by letter so many years ago was just as real to her this day, almost fifteen years after his death.

So, too, I thought is God's message of love for us which continues, warm and deep, centuries after the writing. As we reread God's Word, we are reminded again and again of God's love.

 Thank you, Lord, for your written Word that tells of your everlasting love for us. Help us to communicate your love to others.

Make a copy of 1 Corinthians 13. Read it daily until you have memorized it.

■ FAITH OF GENERATIONS

2 Tim. 1:1-7: "I have been reminded of your sincere faith, which first lived in your grandmother Lois and in your mother Eunice and, I am persuaded, now lives in you also" (v. 5).

Somebody up there must like you," nurse Linda quipped as she gently towel-dried the tender, swollen areas on Marty's body. The 19-year-old was brought to the emergency room last evening after a fight in a nearby parking lot. Abrasions and contusions covered his face, hands and arms. His left eye was swollen shut. Knowing the night nurse's observations had indicated no evidence of the suspected brain concussion, Linda added, "It could have been a lot worse, you know."

Obviously in pain, emotionally and physically, Marty studied her face a minute, then quietly asked, "I don't know you very well, but would you do something for me?"

Without hesitation, Linda said, "Of course, what?"

"Nurse," he paused, "would you pray for me that I may know the Lord?"

As a committed Christian, Linda was grateful for this opportunity. "I'll be glad to, Marty."

After affirming her own faith, she prayed with Marty and heard him express his desire to follow Christ. He remained thoughtful a moment, then smiled, "You know, nurse, my grandmother used to pray for me."

The genuine faith reflected in the prayers of a loving grandmother served as a lodestar to guide Marty to Christ.

 For the sincere faith and prayers of those who are rooted in you, we thank you, Lord.

Whose faith has been an inspiration to you?

14

■ A CUP OF WATER

Mark 9:33-41: "I tell you the truth, anyone who gives you a cup of water in my name because you belong to Christ will certainly not lose his reward" (v. 41).

Our primary aim is to relieve the major caregiver," Rachel explained in discussing her 11 years as a hospice volunteer. Surely this is a "cup of water" ministry.

The official hospice team includes a coordinator, nursing coordinator, chaplain, and social worker. They meet with the patient and family of the terminally ill patient. Based on the doctor's recommendation and the request of patient and family, the type of assistance needed is noted.

"I have *never* gone to the hospital or to a hospice patient that I haven't felt like getting down on my knees and thanking God that I am *able* to help someone else. Being able is a responsibility and a privilege.

"One man, for whom I could do nothing but offer water in a spoon every half hour, asked about a verse in John," she said. "I read one, then another. Finally, I read the entire gospel of John to him. When I finished reading the last verse, he sighed, saying, 'That was beautiful.' He died that night. I was so glad that I was able to do that for him."

 Grant a special blessing, Lord, on those who give comfort to people whose lives are measured in days and hours.

If interested and able, consider hospice volunteer work.

■ COMPASSION ON ALL

Psalm 145: "The Lord is good to all; he has compassion on all he has made" (v. 9).

When Jesus walked on earth, leprosy was the dread illness. Lepers were cast out of society. People feared their illness. But Jesus repeatedly showed compassion.

Today victims of AIDS (acquired immune deficiency syndrome) have suffered similar stigma. Even though the disease is now proven nontransmittable if reasonable precautions are followed, the AIDS victims are greatly feared. Public anxiety has caused rejection in medical transportation, hospitalization and even mortuary care after death. Tragically, the fear may even supercede compassion in family ties.

One victim, slow in speech and movement after battling a daily fever for over a year, said, "I want to live. I am by nature a happy person. I always have been, but this life is the ultimate in desolation and isolation. The personal rejection is far more devastating than the disease."

Surely such a victim must feel the sting of Isaiah's words in reference to Christ: "He was despised and rejected of men, a man of sorrows and familiar with suffering. Like one from whom men hide their faces."

 Lord, help us, that our compassion for those who suffer may make a difference for good.

Approach your daily work with the question, How would Christ treat this person?

■ BROTHERLY LOVE

1 John 3:16-20: "If anyone has material possessions and sees his brother in need but has no pity on him, how can the love of God be in him" (v. 17).

After several years of nursing in metropolitan and suburban hospitals, Lynn accepted a position with the public health department of a major city. Low-income tenants, street people, and refugees presented problems of basic medical needs. Lynn developed a genuine caring for all of them, but felt particularly drawn toward the refugees.

Consequently she signed up for a tour of American Red Cross duty in an Asian refugee camp. "It changed my life totally," she said. "Two years later I signed up for service in another area. When you see these gentle people who have had everything taken away and two-thirds of their own people killed, materialism seems unimportant.

"What a strong bond we felt when world citizens of Ireland, Japan and the United States worked together to relieve suffering and starvation. We listened to the stories which refugees begged to tell. Stories of persecution and fear, so horrible they had to be told. The tellings were a catharsis to relieve the accumulated memories. As workers we had to build an imaginary shell around ourselves to protect our own mental health. Once I was a part of their lives, I could never forget them."

 Move our hearts, Lord, that we may reach out to the destitute, the homeless, the needy in heart and soul.

What opportunities are open for service to those less fortunate in your community?

17

■ LAUGHTER AND JOY

Ps. 126:1-3: "Our mouths were filled with laughter, our tongues with songs of joy" (v. 2).

Have you ever been in a room where someone has laughed so heartily that it made you start to chuckle? Usually when the laughter subsides, a mellow, relaxed feeling remains. Tensions and worries evaporate.

The psalms frequently refer to laughter and joy. In Ps. 126:2 we read: "Our mouths were filled with laughter, our tongues with songs of joy;" in Ps. 66:1: "Shout with joy to God, all the earth!" Such verses often follow expressions of sorrow, pain, adversity, or persecution.

A hospital senior treatment unit frequently dealt with people who had suffered many losses through death of a loved one from physical limitations, or from a move from their home of many years. Feelings of powerlessness, inadequacy, and low self-worth were common. Although treatment encompassed all aspects of need, music and games tended to gradually lift spirits and restore their enjoyment of life. They sang familiar old hymns and melodies; they listened to and shared in poetry of yesteryear. Each activity triggered happy memories and lightened their hearts. Slowly hope was restored and life seemed worth living. Laughter and joy are blessings for everyone.

 Thank you, Lord, for the glints of joy and laughter which sparkle like diamonds through the occasional clouds of our daily life.

Take time to recall special happy moments in your life. Share them with someone you care about.

■ GOD OF COMPASSION AND COMFORT

2 Cor. 1:3-7: "Praises be to God. . . . who comforts us in our troubles, so that we can comfort those in any trouble with the comfort we ourselves have received from God" (vv. 3-4).

When Satan afflicted Job with sores from the top of his head to the soles of his feet, Job became deeply discouraged. When his friend, Eliphaz, saw Job, he wept. He could not speak to Job, because he saw how great his suffering was. Finally Eliphaz asked, "If someone ventures a word with you, will you become impatient?"

Job was a man whom the Lord described as "blameless and upright, a man who fears God and shuns evil" (Job 2:3). But Job's patience was severely tested. What did he feel? Anger? Discouragement? Bitterness? Who could approach him?

Perhaps some of the deepest healing comes today, not through modern technological advances, but through support groups of all kinds. People who have endured soul pain can later be of great assistance to a person in a similar position. Whether touched by Alzheimer's disease, stillborn death, cancer, or mental illness, if in their trial people have been supported, they can in turn be a great solace to others.

 Help us, Lord, to be encouragement to others because our consolation in trouble has come from you.

Inform yourself of support groups available for all situations to empower yourself as an advocate, when possible, for those in pain.

■ WHOM DO WE TRUST?

Hebrews 2:13: "And again, 'I will put my trust in him.' "

Worries and fears may hinder us from putting our trust in God. Likewise our patients' concerns may block our efforts in helping them until they place their trust in us.

One night I was making frequent checks on Anna, our new patient. "She speaks Polish, very little English," the evening nurse had reported. "Her vision is so poor, she gets confused. We put a waistband restraint on her. Watch her closely."

Later, street light from Anna's window revealed her tossing and turning, then trying to get out of bed. Quickly I reached her bedside and supported her until her short legs reached the floor.

It was 12:30 A.M. She needed rest, but how could I communicate with her? Tilting my head onto my folded hands, I feigned sleep, then asked, "You—no sleep?" She stared blankly. I placed a clear red sleeping pill in a tiny paper cup, pointing first to her, then to the capsule. I pleaded, "Anna, you take?"

Her eyes studied my face, the capsule, then me again.

Slowly a nod of her head and the words, "Yah, I take. I trust you." Then, thrusting her forefinger upward, added, "*God first!* Then you."

 Thank you, Lord, that when worries and fears overwhelm us, we may put our trust in you.

Memorize 1 Peter 5:7, "Cast all your anxiety on him because he cares for you."

■ FRAGILITY OF LIFE

Ps. 103:15-16: "As for man, his days are like grass, he flourishes like a flower in the field; the wind blows over it and it is gone."

In nursing I see the emotional pain in the loss of a loved one. The illness may have been rather brief—perhaps from a rapidly spreading malignancy, an irreparable heart problem, or a grossly deficient immune system.

Other families face the trauma of sudden death through car accidents, power line work, post-surgical thrombosis, heart attacks. A vibrant, healthy person has suddenly died. Those who mourn are faced with their own mortality. Our days are "like grass"—the wind blows over it and it is gone.

Imagine the young mother who finds her apparently healthy infant lifeless when she goes to pick him up in the morning. Sudden infant death syndrome, the silent thief of life, has claimed her child.

Days and moments are precious. We treasure memories of happy times and feel a need for life to be meaningful. We value words of support, encouragement, appreciation, and love. We shun destructive and discouraging words which may compound a person's burden of concerns, for our "days are like grass . . . the wind blows over it and it is gone."

 In each of our personal contacts today, keep us mindful of the preciousness of life, Lord.

Make a special effort to praise a colleague, thank a worker, or encourage a family member today.

■ COME TO A QUIET PLACE

Mark 6:30-32:   "Then, because so many people were coming and going that they did not even have a chance to eat, he said to them, 'Come with me by yourselves to a quiet place and get some rest' " (v. 31).

When work pressures are constant and unyielding, when you are physically spent and your heart is heavy with cares of your own and others, you may need to do as Jesus advised, "Come with me by yourselves to a quiet place and rest."

Jesus was so engrossed in teaching and healing the many people who came to him, that he felt he had to get away to rest. With the disciples he went by boat to a solitary place.

Where do you go for quiet, solitude, and rest? It may not be far, simply a place apart from the whirl of daily schedules. Therapeutically, it should totally separate you from connectedness to your work.

Restoration of body and soul often comes to people who can be in touch with nature. Perhaps by a lake, or woods. It may help you to cast worry aside as you hear the birds chatter and sing, remembering Jesus' care of them. They do not sow or reap or store food in barns, yet they are provided for. "Are you not much more valuable than they?" Jesus asks (Matt. 6:26).

 Thank you, Lord, for rest which refreshes us for work.

Review Psalm 23 with a focus on "he restores my soul."

22

■ LOVE YOUR ENEMIES

Luke 6:27-31: "But I tell you who hear me: Love your enemies, do good to those who hate you, bless those who curse you, pray for those who mistreat you" (v. 27).

Rose, now an Armenian nurse, had in childhood many reasons to resent the Turks. They were given control over her country after World War I and severely persecuted Armenian Christians.

Rose's grandfather was killed by the occupation forces, and one of her aunts was sold as a slave to a traveling caravan, just like Joseph. After a three-year search, her family found her in India, still a slave.

Rose's family fled to Beruit, where she studied nursing. She had worked as a nurse in the Mediterranean area, but it was when she was on duty in Cairo, Egypt, that her Christian faith was strongly tested.

Rose knew, instinctively, that one of her patients was of the Turkish race. Without hesitation she gave him the same gentle care as her other patients. Suddenly, he looked up at her and said, "How can it be, that you, an Armenian, can give me such tender, loving care, considering what my ancestors did to your ancestors?"

"But there is a higher love," Rose said, "a love our Lord taught us. He taught us to love even our enemies and to show genuine love and concern for all people."

 Lord, thank you for love demonstrated by Rose, whose ancestors learned of it from the very lips of your apostle Paul.

Do you pray for those who have treated you badly?

■ WHEN CHAPLAINCY STANDS BY

Isa. 43:1-5: "Fear not, for I have redeemed you; I have called you by name; you are mine. When you pass through the waters, I will be with you" (vv. 1-2).

To listen, to share, to comfort the spirit and to bring a measure of peace. This is how one chaplain described his work.

"We find it necessary to wait until a person is ready," the chaplain explained. We sort of stand on the street corner waiting until patients, family or staff members need a person to share their worries, anxieties or grief.

People express their deepest faith and their hope. They rely on us as spiritual pilgrims accompanying them on the most intense and honest of journeys.

People of all ages, coming to the hospital, have varied backgrounds and experiences. They need to be accepted as they are. They need to be the person they want to be. Chaplains try to assure patients that the Lord understands our failings and fears. He forgives and brings us peace.

In a sense the chaplains reassure a person in the words of the Lord in Isaiah: "Fear not, for I have redeemed you" (v. 1).

 Thank you, Lord, for chaplains who stand by us in our most fragile moments and reassure us that you are with us in our struggles, sorrows and joys.

When have you "walked through the waters" with a friend, relative, or acquaintance? Who has stood beside you?

■ SO NEAR, YET SO FAR, FROM HELP

John 5:2-9: " 'Sir,' the invalid replied, 'I have no
one to help me into the pool' " (v. 7).

Imagine an invalid so close to the source of healing
yet not able to get into the pool on his own power. In
the tragic disease of alcoholism we frequently see a
similar situation. Though deeply affected and inwardly
miserable, denial is so strong that the afflicted cannot,
on his own, reach the place where help is available.

Today, with caring, confrontive and supportive help,
lives are turned around in chemical dependency
treatment centers. Like the invalid at the pool of
healing at Bethesda, the alcoholic may want to be
healed, but needs someone to help him to get "into
the pool."

Today, through the combined efforts of a chemical
dependency counselor and those affected by
alcoholism, an alcoholic may be firmly, but lovingly
confronted with the reality of alcoholism and be
encouraged to go into treatment.

Through God's grace, the afflicted can look to Jesus
in faith, and be healed. In compassion, Christ can heal
and restore a troubled soul.

  Lord, increase our awareness of those who
desperately need your healing touch. Help us
to bring them to your healing power.

**Be keenly aware of the pain suffered by the alcohol-
afflicted persons, and those whose lives are
tormented by their illness.**

■ HEALING WORDS

Prov. 12:18: "Reckless words pierce like a sword, but the tongue of the wise brings healing."

The alcoholic, when faced with the painful reality of his drinking problem, can no longer cover actions with lies. Direct confrontation may be jarring, but leads to truth and healing.

If either the alcoholic or those affected by the illness seeks counseling before reaching the treatment stage, the counselor must understand chemical dependency or have an accurate knowledge of the dynamics of alcoholism. If not, the afflicted may unwittingly be further enabled to continue his downward path and those who love him may feel added burdens of guilt, self-punishment and a battered ego. Well meaning, but uninformed counselors, do not bring the words of healing which are so desperately needed.

"Now I see what is happening," an affected person said after seeking out a chemical dependency counselor. "It is like putting on a pair of glasses. Sometimes, when I thought I was helping, I was actually enabling the problem to continue. And the words, which hurt so much, are part of the behavior."

 Thank you, Lord, for wise counselors who bring words of healing to troubled souls.

If confronted with the problem of alcoholism, make a special effort to help the afflicted and those affected by seeking the aid of a chemical dependency counselor.

■ ANGEL REDEFINED

"Psalm 91: "He will call upon me, and I will answer him" (v. 15).

My childhood image of an angel was a tall person-figure with snow white wings. When I was a 21-year-old student nurse, a middle-aged woman shattered that image.

"Mornin', honey," she drawled as I stepped into her room, my arms loaded with supplies.

"Time to change your dressings, Mrs. Jackson," I explained as I pulled back the covers, removed layers of gauze, and exposed a gaping ulcerated area. Viewing the hideous sight, I had to stifle a spontaneous gasp.

As I started gently to cleanse the area, I heard what sounded like the voice of an angel: "He who dwells in the shelter of the Most High will rest in the shadow of the Almighty."

The words, clearly articulated, seemed to come from the depths of her soul. A quick glance revealed her tranquil face, her closed eyes, her halo of silver-flecked hair.

"He will call upon me and I will answer him; I will be with him in trouble. I will deliver him and honor him." While I worked, her words poured forth until she had eloquently rendered all of Psalm 91.

Thank you, Lord, for the promise that you will answer us when we call upon you. And bless, Lord, your "angels," who remind us of that promise.

When has someone appeared as an angel in your life bringing you words of encouragement, hope or blessing?

27

■ THE IF-ONLYS OF GRIEF

2 Sam. 18:33—19:4: "The king was shaken. . . .'Oh, my son Absalom! My son, my son Absalom! If only I had died instead of you' " (v. 33).

David's grief over his son was so devastating that he said, "If only I had died instead of you—"

How often, following a death, a grief-stricken loved one may say, "If only—" For them it might be if only I had noticed the symptoms earlier, if only I had taken him to another doctor or clinic, or if only I had spent more time with him.

Imagine the young father, highly skilled in pediatric emergencies, who leaves the joyous family gathering in his home to check on his napping infant son only to find the child is a victim of sudden infant death syndrome. His if-only groans are eased through the loving and understanding support of others who have suffered such a painful loss. Slowly, he realizes he could not have changed the outcome.

As caregivers we should be attuned to the if-only feelings which may follow the death of a loved one, that our words may not contribute toward any feelings of guilt, but rather respond to their pain.

 Give us heart, Lord, to empathize with those who suffer a loss. Grant us words of healing for their aching hearts.

Memorize Gal. 6:2, "Carry each other's burdens, and in this way you will fulfill the law of Christ."

■ PRAYER AT DAYBREAK

Mark 1:35-39:   "Very early in the morning, while it was still dark, Jesus got up, left the house and went off to a solitary place, where he prayed" (v. 35).

Jesus often withdrew from a crowd and went to a quiet spot to pray. Here we read that he left the house while it was still dark and went off to a solitary place. He got away from distractions to focus on prayer.

Morning prayers are like words written on an empty slate. In the still of the morning, we may seek God's direction for our day. We may ask blessings on our loved ones and our work. We may bring concerns before the Lord, and pray that our lives may reflect the love of Christ to those we meet.

One nursing home nurse said, "Each morning when I enter this door, I pray that whatever I do for the least of these, I will do as unto Christ."

Another nurse said, "On days when I leave home just before sunrise, I allow time to pause at the southern edge of our neighborhood lake. As the sky begins to lighten, it reflects onto the silvery water. Even as the sky becomes pink, brightening the rippled lake, I ask God to guide my actions for the day. I feel the beauty of God's creation and am uplifted."

 Thank you, Lord, for the freshness of this day. Be with us in all we do.

Start each day with prayer. Be specific. List names of persons and concerns for daily use.

■ BE NOT ANXIOUS

Phil. 4:6-7: "Do not be anxious about anything, but in everything, by prayer and petition, with thanksgiving, present your requests to God" (v. 6).

Can we change anything by worry? Christ asks, "Who of you by worrying can add a single hour to his life?" (Matt. 6:27). He reminds us how our heavenly Father cares for the lilies of the field and the birds of the air.

Our anxiety level can rise readily simply by listening to the world newscast, not to mention numerous other concerns we may have. Some of Christ's last words to his disciples were in John 16:33 where he says, "I have told you these things, so that *in me* you may have peace. In this world you will have trouble. But take heart! I have overcome the world."

Alvin N. Rogness, former seminary president, stated in his book *Forgiveness and Confession,* "The absence of trust and the presence of anxiety is man's deepest offense against a God who loves him with an everlasting love."

"Do not be anxious about anything," Paul wrote, "but, in everything, by prayer and petition, with thanksgiving, present your requests to God." Approach God with thankful and trusting hearts, knowing that in God's wisdom and with God's power we will be granted that which is best for us.

 Grant, Lord, that our faith may rest not in human beings, but in your power and will.

Recall God's provision for Moses through his wilderness wanderings, for Abraham by sparing his son, and for Joseph who was cast away by his brothers yet later became in charge of Egypt where he had been taken.

■ HEALING THROUGH FORGIVENESS

1 John 1:8-10: "If we confess our sins, he is faithful and just and will forgive us our sins, and purify us from all unrighteousness" (v. 10).

Sin comes in many forms and manners. Careless, hurtful words which cut, pierce or offend are sins as well as the senseless, violent taking of a life. Thoughts or behavior which is contrary to the glory or character of God is sin. It is also sin to commit an offense against God's laws. James even says that anyone "who knows the good he ought to do and doesn't do it, sins" (James 4:17).

Paul says, "for *all* have sinned and fall short of the glory of God" (Rom. 3:23). Whether by thought, word, deed or omission of doing what we ought, we sin daily. We need to daily ask for the forgiveness which we are promised.

Occasionally depressed people under psychiatric care respond poorly in spite of repeated medication attempts. Guilt, often deep and longstanding, may underlie the heaviness of a heart. If a therapist, psychiatric technician, nurse, or chaplain can help the patient release pent-up thoughts which lead to confession and forgiveness, healing may begin. Like the debridement of a wound comes the word of our Lord, "Though your sins are like scarlet, they shall be as white as snow" (Isa. 1:18).

 Help us to see our sins, Lord, and ask forgiveness, that renewed we may be a strength to others.

He became what we are that he might make us what he is (St. Athanasius).

■ WHEN DECEIT DESTROYS

Rom. 16:17-19: "Watch out for those who put obstacles in the way that are contrary to the teaching you have learned. . . . By smooth talk and flattery they deceive the minds of naive people" (vv. 17-18).

In these verses Paul appealed to Christians in Rome to hold to their teachings. Beware, he said, of people who may lead you astray by smooth talk and flattery. He added, "I want you to be wise about what is good, and innocent about what is evil."

Beth Ann, a church social worker in a large city, walks the streets and goes wherever juvenile prostitutes spend their time. They are young girls who have been deceived by the smooth talk of young males.

A charming fellow calls to a girl walking nearby, "Hey, you, can I talk to you a second?" She pretends she does not hear so he teases, "Too good to speak?" Still no response.

"Prejudiced, huh?" Now she reacts. She has been taught to be nice. She listens as his flattering words hold her attention.

Suddenly she says she should go home. "Oh, you don't *have* to," he says. Before leaving she may agree to meet him again. Soon she moves in with him, then they need money and the slide downward leads to prostitution.

Beth Ann, a visible presence of Christ's love, redirects the girls to daily living and job skill training.

 Lord, keep us firm in your teachings that we may not be deceived by false precepts.

Pray that our young people may be strengthened in their faith.

32

■ GOD, GIVER OF LIFE

Acts 17:24-28: "The God who made the world and everything in it is the Lord of heaven and earth. . . . he himself gives all men life and breath. . . . 'We are his offspring'" (vv. 24-25, 28).

During a Bible study discussion on life values, a doctor told of his father, then in his mid-eighties, who recently made and put into place a marker for the grave of his son. The child had died at birth. In the twilight of his life, the father's very actions honored as a gift his child's long ago brief life.

Today, when laws permit abortions as late as the sixth month of pregnancy, we hear mind-boggling statistics about the number of abortions performed. We do not know the soul-searching and heartache which may accompany many abortions. But the alarming number suggests a casual attitude toward the life of an unborn child.

Life is a gift from God "who made the world and everything in it." God gives to all life and breath. What a significant gift!

Nurses and doctors who attend critically ill patients, see the amazing tenacity of those who cling to life in spite of great and often prolonged suffering. They know the preciousness of each breath.

In Jer. 1:5 we read the Lord's words: "Before I formed you in the womb I knew you, before you were born I set you apart."

 For the precious gift of life, we thank you, Lord. May we live it to your honor.

In what concrete ways may we show reverence for life as a gift from God?

33

■ TEACH US WHAT TO SAY

Exod. 4:10-17: "Who gave man his mouth?. . . Is it not I, the Lord? Now go; I will help you speak and will teach you what to say" (vv. 11-12).

The Lord spoke to Moses when he was feeling very inadequate for the task of leading his people. "Oh, Lord, I have never been eloquent—" Moses said. "I am slow of speech and tongue." Moses' faith in God was strong, but he had difficulty expressing himself to others.

How often have we felt inadequate to share our faith in God? A hospice nurse who attended many dying patients shared her thoughts regarding how we can be supportive.

1. Convey an openness to share faith questions and beliefs with patient and family.

2. Let the patient know that doubt, questions, and anger are normal feelings. It helps to share them with someone they trust.

3. Many patients feel more comfortable sharing their thoughts and feelings if they know the nurse *also* is a Christian.

4. A small gesture—touching a shoulder, holding a hand, or telling a patient God is with him may be very meaningful.

5. Read a favorite Bible passage.

6. Offer to pray with the patient and family.

Dear Lord, when we feel inadequate for the task, help us to speak words of healing.

Remember God's words to Moses: "I will help you speak."

■ PRAYER POWER

James 5:13-16: "The prayer of a righteous man is powerful and effective" (v. 16).

Here James primarily addressed prayer for the healing of the sick. He said the prayer offered in faith will make a sick person well, and urged people to pray for each other so they might be healed.

In Numbers 12, we read how Moses cried out to the Lord to heal Miriam, who had been stricken with leprosy. She was healed.

In Numbers 21, we read how God, angered by the Israelite's murmurings against him, sent venomous snakes as punishment. The people were bitten. Many died. When the people confessed their sin and pleaded with Moses, he interceded. He prayed that the Lord would take the snakes away.

Then the Lord commanded Moses to make a bronze snake, and put it on a tall pole for all to see. Anyone who was bitten, could look at the bronze snake and be healed. Moses interceded for them and God provided the opportunity, but it took their act of faith, looking up to the bronze snake, to be healed.

We know prayers of faith are offered today. We see people healed. Sometimes the miracles are obscured by modern technology, but nonetheless, they are God-given miracles.

 As our daily work touches the lives of your children, Lord, we pray that they may look up to you in faith.

What miracles of healing have you seen? in body? in soul? in mind?

35

■ A WILLINGNESS TO GIVE

John 15:9-17: "Greater love has no one than this, that one lay down his life for his friends" (v. 13).

Patricia, a nurse in a small pediatric unit, told of the day she was on duty when six-year-old Todd was admitted. His four-year-old sister, Jenny, was to undergo major cardiac surgery and needed extra blood available. Because Todd and Jenny shared a rare, genetic blood condition, Todd was scheduled for a phlebotomy, to allow a donation of his blood.

A veteran of multiple surgeries, Todd knew the hospital and the nurses well; he stoically submitted to the brief procedure. He remained grim and silent as Jenny climbed up on his bed, thumb in mouth, clutching her favorite doll.

Half an hour later Todd and Jenny remained still in the room as the doctor carefully explained Jenny's procedure to their parents. Nurse Geri monitored the blood flow and Patricia brought Todd beverages.

Todd seemed to be seeking Geri's attention when, in a pause of the doctor's speech, his quavery voice asked, "Geri, excuse me, but how long will it be now?"

"Well, Todd, what do you mean?"

"I mean—how much time before I die after all my blood is gone out of me?"

Leaden silence filled the room as each person realized that Todd willingly gave his blood for his sister fully believing that he would die!

 Thank you, Lord, for loving hearts willing to give, even life.

Recall the words of Isaiah, "And a little child shall lead them" (11:6).

■ A LOVE THAT DOES NOT FAIL

Lam. 3:19-24: "Because of the Lord's great love we are not consumed, for his compassions never fail" (v. 22).

Have you encountered a life situation which seems unbearable? Have you experienced the feeling of total helplessness when you or someone you love endures great pain and you are powerless to change the situation?

An elderly friend said her Norwegian father explained to her a prayer which upheld her in difficult times. It read: *"Sorg, o kjare Fader du."* "From the depths of our souls," he said, "we plead, 'Oh Father, I do not know how to take care of this. May I leave it in your hands?' "

We suffer with another but are not consumed, because God's love never fails.

Martha, a county nurse, saw the desire to relieve another's distress demonstrated by employees of a health-care facility. She described the staff as "the most compassionate people I have ever known." The facility cared for victims of Huntington's chorea in which muscle control is gradually lost. Because swallowing is a problem and arms may fling about, all personnel participate in one-to-one feeding at meal times. "Food spatters so badly that the room has to be literally hosed down after the meal, yet these workers approach each patient with a caring which is heart-warming to see," Martha said.

 Thank you, Lord, for your great love which gives us strength to continue when life seems difficult.

Remember, "His compassions never fail."

■ AN ACT OF LOVE

John 19:38-42: "Taking Jesus' body, the two of them wrapped it, with the spices, in strips of linen. This was in accordance with Jewish burial customs" (v. 40).

As I wash the body and say the blessings, it's in the back of my mind all the time: These men working with me are the men who will take care of me in the same way someday—someday soon."

The 78-year-old member of the Jewish synagogue in Minneapolis explained the purpose of the Chevra Kevod Hamet program, the Society to Honor the Dead.

Members see the practice as a matter of dignity for each person. No embalming. No cosmetics. Nothing to retard natural body deterioration.

They feel a strong sense of family as they take over when a member dies. This means full responsibility for body preparation, wrapping the body in a plain shroud, assisting with the family's immediate needs, and around-the-clock vigil until the burial in a plain pine box.

One lad, after keeping vigil at his grandfather's side, said, "I sat for two hours reading and reflecting on my grandfather's life and death. I think it helped me look at death in the right perspective."

One member said, "It's such a loving act to do, and all the more beautiful because the person you do it for cannot pay you back."

 As caregivers, Lord, we dedicate our acts of love to your glory.

Watch for opportunities to act out of love for others.

■ FAITH COMES BY HEARING

Rom. 10:17: "Consequently, faith comes from hearing the message, and the message is heard through the word of Christ."

Hilda had not spoken a word or responded in any way since she fell into a coma two weeks earlier. Yet when her pastor stood beside her bed reading Psalm 23, her lips moved silently in perfect unison. "The Lord is my shepherd. . . . Even though I walk through the valley of the shadow of death, I will fear no evil, for you are with me. . . ."

Faith-affirming, comforting words learned in childhood came forth when life appeared to be ebbing away.

As caregivers we may share Scripture to uplift burdened hearts, comfort those who mourn, to allay fears and discouragement, to assure forgiveness to contrite hearts, and to join in praise and thanksgiving.

When enduring trials, Nah. 1:7: "The Lord is good, a refuge in times of trouble. He cares for those who trust him."

When fearful or discouraged, Deut. 31:8: "The Lord himself goes before you and will be with you; he will never forsake you. Do not be discouraged."

For those who mourn, John 5:24: "Whoever hears my word and believes him who sent me has eternal life."

For the forgiveness of sin, 1 John 1:9: "If we confess our sins, he is faithful and just and will forgive us our sins, and purify us from all unrighteousness."

 Lord, guide us in sharing your words of promise and hope with those hungry to hear them.

Memorize Scripture for use in helping situations.

■ WHOM DO WE FEAR?

Matt. 10:28: "Do not be afraid of those who kill the body but cannot kill the soul."

Fear prevailed, remittant and recurring, in the Cambodian camp where Jan served with the American Red Cross in Thailand. Nursing was primitive. Charcoal fires boiled the water for sterilization of equipment.

Refugees crowded into fenced areas. Fear gripped them, especially at night when they frequently heard gunfire. Sadistic, often drunken guards sitting at high surveilance posts shot anyone coming out of a bamboo hut.

One doctor, having to physically restrain a mental patient until he could reach the hospital barracks, feared for his own life. Guards, he learned, were informed of his action and might misinterpret his intentions.

Few of us have lived in such a tense situation. Surely fear is a normal reaction. The doctor feared not only for his life, but because he was on call for 1000 refugees that night. What if something happened to him? We, too, may feel obligations unfulfilled.

Christ says we should not fear death. As Christians we live with the promise of eternal life. But Christ does say we *should* fear those who would kill the soul. Fear those who could destroy your faith in God.

 Make us aware of soul-destroying behavior, Lord, that we may protect ourselves and others from it.

Do you feel a sense of fear for children when you see excessive violence on TV, a flaunting of immoral behavior or irreverance toward God?

■ GOD WILL SUSTAIN YOU

Isa. 46:3-7: "Even to your old age and gray hairs I am he, I am he who will sustain you. I have made you and I will carry you" (v. 4).

Kind words often come from most unexpected sources. So it was one day when Laurie came to visit her mother at the Pine Ridge Health Center. As a public health nurse, Laurie had frequently faced the problems of long-term care. She was grateful for the excellent and loving care which her own mother received.

But visits were increasingly difficult as her mother's memory failed. Communication became only words of reality testing.

Today, Laurie walked heavy-hearted toward the door. Just inside, she saw Kate beside her cleaning cart.

"Hi, Laurie!" Kate smiled. "It is always so good to see you." Then, stepping forward, she added, "It must be hard to see your mother this way."

Warmed by Kate's concern, Laurie replied, "Yes, it surely is. I guess, though the hardest part is knowing all the emotional pain my mother has suffered—the lingering death of my sister, dad's sudden death, then my brother. During all of her trials she always had God to call on for strength, and she did. But now," Laurie hesitated, "it almost seems she has forgotten God."

"But, Laurie," Kate urged, "you know God has not forgotten her!"

 Thank you, Lord, for the promise that you will sustain your own even into old age.

Memorize Isa. 46:4, "I have made you and will carry you."

■ STRENGTH THROUGH UNITY

Eph. 4:1-16: "Then we will no longer be infants, tossed . . . by waves, and blown . . . by every wind of teaching and by the cunning and craftiness of men in their deceitful scheming" (v. 14).

Paul pleaded for unity that each may grow in faith and knowledge, therefore making strong the body of Christ. He warned of cunning and crafty people who destroy faith.

Shortly after two United States Navy men were charged with passing highly classified information to the Soviet Union, a retired nurse was telling about her experiences as a nurse during World War II.

"At first we were billeted in the homes of English families. Quonsets were quickly erected as hospitals.

"I will never forget the drone of a skyful of airplanes as they left for the D-Day invasion in France."

After a thoughtful moment, she continued, "Our unit was supposed to receive only the wounded who could be rehabilitated within three months, but in the rush we received every type of injury."

Another pause, then, looking up, her voice broke as she asked, "How can a man *deceive* his country?" She understood the weakening effect resulting from such deception and could not comprehend such behavior.

If we study God's Word and seek God's guidance, God will help us stand firm against those who would undermine our beliefs.

 Protect us from those who would destroy our faith, Lord, that we may not be tossed about in uncertainty.

Feast on daily Bible reading and prayer for strength and nourishment of your faith.

■ GOODNESS: GIFT OF THE SPIRIT

Eph. 5:8-14: "Now you are light in the Lord. Live as children of light (for the fruit of light consists in all goodness, righteousness, and truth)" (vv. 8-9).

Marcy, a nurse on temporary assignment to a nursing home, was aware of Rita's difficult behavior. She was mean. She liked to walk behind people and push them. After a rather serious incident two aides decided to secure Rita to her chair. As they anchored the ties, she screamed, "You devils!"

Just then Marcy entered the room. At the sight of her, Rita quieted, looked directly into her eyes and said, "But *you*, nurse, are light."

What is different about children of light? Paul says the fruit of the light is goodness, righteousness and truth.

John says that in him (God) was life; and that light was the light of men (1:4).

Many people have reported "threshold experiences," having crossed the line between life and death. In each case they relate the sensation of the presence of a light. One, a doctor, said there is no word to describe brilliance that intense. His experience changed his life for good.

Having the light of God in us, we do what is morally right and true, what is pleasing to God.

 May the light of your goodness shine through us, Lord, in what we say and do.

"Let your light shine before men, that they may see your good deeds and praise your Father in heaven" (Matt. 5:16).

■ A WORD APTLY SPOKEN

Prov. 25:11: "A word aptly spoken is like apples of gold in settings of silver."

It was such a happy occasion," the retired nursing instructor said regarding her eightieth birthday party. "In all, I received 100 cards from all over—former pupils, nurses, sisters, but I guess the one from the daughter of an old classmate meant the most to me.

"When I was sorting through my photo collection before coming to the nursing home, I discovered her parents' wedding picture. Her parents had died so I felt she was the one who should have the photograph. I mailed it to her. You see her parents had severed contact with her when they did not approve of the man she married. Now when she sent me the birthday card she added the most touching note of thanks. 'It meant far more to me than you can imagine,' she wrote. 'As you know my parents and I had no contact for years. They had never given me a picture, so you can see why it now means so much to me.' "

An act of kindness brought warm words of gratitude, words aptly spoken, like apples of gold in settings of silver.

We can use words to encourage coworkers, to uplift the downhearted, to express appreciation for a supervisor, to inform apprehensive presurgical patients, to reconcile staff differences, to bless our fellow human beings. All can be words aptly spoken.

 Guard our thoughts, Lord, that our words may honor you.

Memorize Ps. 19:14, "May the words of my mouth and the meditation of my heart be pleasing in your sight, O Lord."

■ FOR THOSE WHO STAND AT THE BEDSIDE

Rom. 12:9-13: "Love must be sincere. . . . Be devoted to one another in brotherly love. . . . Be joyful in hope, patient in affliction, faithful in prayer" (vv. 9-10, 12).

So how do I deal with my wife's long-term illness, you ask. Well, in many different ways at different times." To the congregation's ministry trainees, the parishioner explained his thoughts and feelings, from the time he first learned his wife's diagnosis of Alzheimer's disease. Now this intelligent and capable lady who had been of great assistance to him in his work rested in a noncommunicative state in a nursing home, rarely showing the vaguest hint of recognition, even to her closest kin.

This parishioner's vigil had been long, disheartening and financially draining. Yet, through it all, he had retained his unwavering faith in God.

"But one truth I have learned," he added, "two sick people do not a well one make." Knowing that maintenance of his mental health was vital to his ability to function well, he took time to enjoy the company of others, time to be uplifted in spirit and mind.

Do we sometimes forget the bedside standers who keep vigil over the loved one's long term illness or debilitating condition?

 Lord, we ask a special blessing on those who stand by a loved one during prolonged illnesses.

Remember a "bedside friend" in prayer daily and be alert for further opportunities for support.

45

■ WE ARE NOT JUDGES

Rom. 14:1-18: "Therefore let us stop passing judgment on one another" (v. 13).

Wherever we are—in hospitals, emergency rooms, counseling centers or in our everyday lives—we brush with people in pain. They may be struggling through a difficult time. Perhaps they seem off track from what we feel is right. Surely we can serve as the ears of Christ when we listen to them, allowing them to unburden their heavy hearts. Or, being the hands of Christ, by directing them to people qualified to help. Or simply caring for their immediate needs without judging their action or behavior.

An obstetrical nurse, herself a mother of three young adults, discussed the concern she felt for single, unwed mothers. "With two parents the task is heavy. How can they manage alone? We make sure the mother has a social worker, we put in a public health referral for her, and give her our phone number so she can call back to us with questions. It always helps to have another ear."

A social worker in a large metropolitan area who deals routinely with cases of family violence, observes, "In the problem-family, anxiety becomes terror and frustration becomes rage. Terror and rage lead to uncontrolled behavior. Family members abuse, physically and verbally, those they love."

 Free us, Lord, from the temptation to judge one another.

Remember Matt. 7:1, "Do not judge, or you too will be judged."

■ TO LIVE A NEW LIFE

Rom. 6:4: "We are therefore buried with him through baptism into death in order that just as Christ was raised from the dead through the glory of the Father, we too may live a new life."

It is not unusual for 13-year-olds to feel self-conscious, insecure, and inadequate for what is expected of them. Teenagers worry about their appearance. Donna was born with a cleft lip. This deformity of her upper lip also pulled her nose askew. Her family could not afford to pay for plastic surgery.

"She doesn't go to parties," her mother said. "She hides behind books."

One day Donna heard the radio announcement about an American team of plastic surgeons, nurses and technicians who donate many hours of service to low-income families. Her heart nearly burst with excitement and hope.

"I want to go. I want to go," she cried.

"I want to wear lipstick on two lips instead of three," she wrote to the doctor who screened patients. "I want to be pretty like my friend."

Imagine the strong hope within her. Imagine her joy when she was selected and the surgery completely transformed her appearance and her personality. The skills of people who cared gave her a new life.

 Bless, Lord, dedicated people who transform external appearances even as you, through Baptism, give us new life in you.

Do you have a skill to offer to someone less fortunate?

■ PRAYER CHANGES LIFE

Heb. 10:19-25: "Let us draw near to God with a sincere heart in full assurance of faith" (v. 22).

As Christian caregivers, we need to draw near to God daily with sincere hearts full of assurance of faith. We may seek guidance, forgiveness, strength, reassurance, but we will also want to praise and give thanks.

Evelyn Underhill said, "Nothing in nature is so lovely and so vigorous, so perfectly at home in its environment, as a fish in the sea. Its surrounding gives it a beauty, quality and power which is not its own. We take it out and at once a poor, limp dull thing, fit for nothing, is gasping away its life. So the soul, sunk in God, living his life of prayer, is supported, filled, transferred in beauty, by a vitality and power which are its own" (*Heirlooms*, Applegarth, p. 207).

Richard Trench's poem captured the essence of prayer when he wrote: "Lord, what a change within us one short hour spent in thy presence will prevail to make, what heavy burdens from our bosoms take, what parched grounds refresh as with a shower!"

How difficult it is to face a day when cares weigh heavily upon our hearts, Paul writes in Phil. 4:6, "Do not be anxious about anything, but in everything, by prayer and petition, with thanksgiving, present your requests to God."

 Thank you, Lord, for the peace which transcends all understanding when we come to you.

Remember, hands folded in prayer open in compassion.

■ A CHEERFUL HEART

Prov. 17:22: "A cheerful heart is good medicine, but a crushed spirit dries up the bones."

As nurses we feel a heavy responsibility in the dispensing of medications. We watch for symptoms of harmful effects. I discovered a way to give a medication with a *beneficial* side effect, a cheerful heart.

Olga, a nursing home resident, was prone to anxiety attacks, usually upon rising. I often diverted her attention by asking about her birthplace in Oslo, Norway. Jokingly, I referred to it as the lutefisk (a favorite Norwegian codfish) capital of the world. Mere mention of Oslo triggered happy memories. Soon she would relax and smile again.

One morning, hyperventilating severely, Olga walked unsteadily toward me. "Nurse," she gasped, "I just cannot make it to breakfast today."

"Oh, Olga," I said as I put one arm around her and reached for her morning medication with the other. "I'm sure this will solve your problem." Then, gazing intently into her blinking eyes, I added, "Do you realize what this capsule is?"

Soberly, she asked, "It's for my heart, isn't it?"

"Well, yes," I conceded, "but it actually is powdered lutefisk straight from Oslo."

"Oh," she laughed, "maybe so."

Chuckling, she returned to her room nearby. Her hyperventilation had greatly eased as I heard her saying, "Lutefisk, eh?" and laughed afresh.

 Dear Lord, help me lift a downcast spirit today with words that lighten the heart.

Search for words of cheerfulness in your speech today.

■ WHEN LOVING IS DIFFICULT

Luke 6:27-36: " 'If you love those who love you, what credit is that to you? Even "sinners" love those who love them' " (v. 32).

Nurses frequently see a person at his worst. He may be in pain, lonely, frightened about a diagnosis, worried about medical costs, or threatened with physical disability. His feelings may erupt in angry outbursts. The closest person, often a nurse, may well be the recipient of his rage.

Anger follows a primary emotion. We must be attuned to the deeper feeling and try to respond to that. Can we relieve the pain, reduce the anxiety, or alleviate the sense of loneliness?

Helen, a diabetic nursing home resident, presented a challenge to staff. Her nightly foot soak became a daily battle. She complained that it was too early or too late, too hot or too cool, too long or too short. If the nurse started to wipe her feet, she might snatch the towel and shout through gritted teeth, "No one does *anything* for me around here."

She complained about tasteless food, no friends, and nothing to do. Knowing she had lost her one close friend and had no nearby family, staff members responded to her screams and accusations with kind firmness. They gave her listening time and gradually urged her into activities of her interest.

Slowly she responded with a new sense of self-worth and self-esteem.

> Lord, help us to love the unloving by reaching out with *your* love, a love beyond ourselves.

Remember Eph. 4:2, "Be completely humble and gentle; be patient, bearing with one another in love."

■ CARING FOR GOD'S TEMPLE

1 Cor. 3:16-17: "Don't you know that you yourselves are God's temple and that God's spirit lives in you? If anyone destroys God's temple, God will destroy him; for God's temple is sacred, and you are that temple."

An emergency room doctor told me that he takes inderal, ten milligrams, three times a day," a reporter said, when involved in a discussion of drug abuse. "When the pressures build and I feel tense," the doctor explained, "It takes the edge off."

Even nurses have occasionally become drug abusers, whether inadvertantly or intentionally. They are a serious threat to the workplace and are endangering their own self-being. Not only do they harm their own bodies, but, most frightening, they may be unable to make safe nursing judgments.

If a doctor or nurse feels such a need to help relax, is it any surprise that football players, entertainers, and others have turned to drug use? The health-care professional *knows* the actions, reactions and potential dangers of each drug. Others may be less informed. After repeated use, they really do not care.

Our bodies are God's temple, a holy place, a habitation for God's spirit. Surely we would not willfully destroy it through abuse by drugs.

> It is an awesome thought, Lord, that our body is your temple. Help us to keep it fit for your dwelling.

Memorize the Serenity Prayer:
God grant us the serenity to accept the things we cannot change, the courage to change the things we can, and the wisdom to know the difference.

■ JOYFUL TELLINGS

Mark 7:31-37: "Jesus commanded them not to tell anyone. But the more he did so, the more they kept talking about it" (v. 36).

Have you ever related a secret to a small child, then cautioned, "Now, don't tell anyone." The child almost bursts with excitement and, not infrequently, explodes the happy news to everyone.

Likewise, when Jesus healed the deaf man with a speech impediment, he asked the people not to tell anyone. But the people, "overwhelmed with amazement," said he had done everything well. They couldn't stop talking about the miracle.

When Marie, an elderly lady in a senior treatment program, was asked where she was from, she named a mid-sized Wisconsin city.

"Oh," her nurse commented, "that is the home of the Carlson Clinic, isn't it?"

"Yes!" Marie answered, quickly reaching for her billfold. "You know about the clinic? I tell you those four brothers, all doctors, are a fine team." Carefully, she produced a small, wilted newspaper clipping. Thrusting it into the nurse's hand, she said, "Look, that's Dr. Richard. *He saved my life!*" It had happened over 40 years earlier, but she kept saying, "I wouldn't be here if it weren't for him."

As the deaf man who was healed and those who saw the miracle, Marie felt the joyful news had to be told.

 May we express our thanks to you, Lord, before others, that they may know what you have done for us.

With whom would you like to share your gratitude story?

■ SONGS TO A HEAVY HEART

Prov. 25:20: "Like . . . vinegar poured on soda, is one who sings songs to a heavy heart."

Tears streamed down the faces of the teenage children as they held their mother in a loving embrace. Divorced, and in her early 40s, the mother had bravely battled her cancer. But then cardiac complications set in. Sadness nearly crushed the children as they faithfully visited her day after day, knowing her time with them was short. Unable to express their feelings, they often sat nearly wordless during their visit.

Margo, the hospice nurse, shared her concern for the family with Carol, a hospice volunteer. How could they help them express their feelings? How abandoned the children must feel. And how painful it must be for the mother to let go of life when she had so much to live for.

They decided to sing hymns for the family when they were all together. They sang of God's love for his children and of how God is always near.

Tears flowed as hearts were touched. Feeling words were spoken. The release of deep pent-up emotions afforded great relief for everyone.

Margo and Carol sang for them many times in the hospital and again at the mother's funeral. Heavy hearts were lightened as the family, through song, were reminded of God's love.

 Thank you, Lord, for the blessings of songs to lighten heavy hearts.

Consider possible use of songs to lighten hearts of those whose lives you touch.

■ AN ANCHOR FOR THE SOUL

Heb. 6:13-20: "We have this hope as an anchor for the soul, firm and secure" (v. 19).

Hope gives us powerful strength. With hope people can survive devastating trauma and deep discouragement. Two definitions of hope, both good, give us keys toward understanding the word. The first is reliance on God's blessing and provision. The second is the expectation of future good.

To me the childhood tellings of Moses' wandering through the wilderness with oft-wayward Israelites presented graphic illustrations of reliance on God's blessing and provision. With hope, Moses endured the many trials and miseries of the long journey.

In illness, we see the power of hope in recovery. Given hope, the patient persists through difficult days. Conversely, once a patient surrenders hope, the doctor's efforts are greatly hindered.

When one doctor told a young couple that their long-awaited baby boy probably would never walk or talk and would be unable to respond to them, they refused to accept his pronouncement. Instead they initiated and persisted in a round-the-clock training program to develop body movements and to stimulate his mind. By their persistent expectation of good, along with their diligent work, their child achieved normal functioning in eighteen months.

> Thank you, Lord, that in you we have hope, an anchor for our souls, firm and secure.

Repeat this blessing today: "May the God of hope fill you with all joy and peace as you trust in him, so that you may overflow with hope by power of the Holy Spirit" (Rom. 15:13).

54

■ WHEN TWO AGREE

Matt. 18:19-20: "Again I tell you that if two of you on earth agree about anything you ask for, it will be done for you by my Father in heaven" (v. 19).

Caroline had suffered from bouts of depression sporadically for years. With medication, and sometimes hospitalization, she had returned to her fully functioning capabilities. She was a charming lady with many interests, many friends, and a zest for life.

This time her depression was so severe that it did not respond to increased dosages of medication. Because she was 80 years old, the doctors were cautious regarding the direction of further treatment. Her lethargy gradually reduced her to bedrest.

Alice, the night nurse, monitored her closely, having observed the Cheyne-Stokes respiratory pattern, so often seen prior to death.

As a last resort, her doctor felt he should try electric shock treatment (EST). Alice sensed the doctor's heavy burden in reaching his decision when he requested the written agreement for treatment be endorsed by a second doctor. She had never before seen a second opinion sought for EST.

Imagine Alice's surprise when she came to work the evening after Caroline's first EST. In the center of a conversational group sat Caroline, actively listening and contributing freely to current discussion.

You know what is good for us, Lord. May we, two together, seek your will.

Have you sought out a partner in prayer?

■ GOD KNOWS OUR HEARTS

1 Kings 8:37-40: "When a prayer or plea is made.
. . . Forgive and act . . . since you know his heart"
(v. 38, 39).

Karen Kaiser Clark conducts seminars in the area of
human relations for hospitals, business, and private
groups. In her book *Where Have All the Children
Gone? Gone to Grown-Ups, Everyone!* a child poses
this question: "I wonder what happens to all the
tears inside of grown-ups. Does the hurting part just
stay inside them?"

Have you ever wondered, "How much does the
heart hold that is invisible to others? Consider the
dedicated worker who accepts extra shifts, rarely uses
sick leave, and puts a plus in all that she does. When
she becomes disenchanted with a job where there are
no expressions of gratitude, praise, or appreciation,
her generally smiling face may cover a heart filled with
anger and resentment. If she does not discuss her
feelings with someone, preferably her supervisor, she
may explode one day and act inappropriately.

How many problems could be averted if people
expressed their feelings appropriately to those by
whom they are affected. But this is difficult, extremely
so for some cultures more than others, and usually
more often for men than for women. But drug abuse,
alcoholism, and acting out behavior might be averted
if feelings are dealt with.

 Lord help us express our concerns properly to
heal the hurts of our hearts.

**Are you able to discuss your feelings with a
supervisor, coworker or friend if it is appropriate?**

■ LONG-LIFE SATISFACTIONS

Ps. 91:14-16: "With long life will I satisfy him and show him my salvation (v. 16).

I saw Angela, one of our board and care residents, frequently in the chapel lounge near her room. Strikingly beautiful, her erect bearing enobled the dignity of her gently etched facial lines and soft blue eyes. Her puff of lightly waved hair reminded me of the proverbial "crown of splendor; it is attained by a righteous life" (Prov. 16:31). Many times I had passed her on my way to others needing attention.

"How are you tonight, Angie?" I asked, clasping her hand in mine.

"Oh, just fine," she smiled, obviously pleased with the personal attention.

"I'm glad to hear that, Angie. Believe it or not, I have had many complaints tonight. I wondered if you might have one, too."

Her smile vanished. Looking thoughtful, she said, "Well, I have spent a lot of time thinking about such things. This is how I figured it out. The Lord has given me over 90 years, and I don't know how much time I have left to live." Her somber look faded. With a twinkle in her eyes, she added, "I've decided that if I spend my time complaining, I might miss out on something good."

 For those you have blessed with a long life and a light heart, we thank you, Lord.

What elderly person represents to you a long satisfied life?

■ WHEN WORDS FAIL

Job 2:7-13: "Then they sat on the ground with him for seven days and seven nights. No one said a word to him, because they saw how great his suffering was" (v. 13).

Think of the worst possible thing that could happen, Mary. Then multiply it times two." Jane's voice, usually strong and clearly expressive, wavered and almost faded away as she related the shattering news. Her only son, disturbed in a troubled marriage, had recently separated from his wife. When he returned to see her, with emotions completely out of control, he shot and killed his wife, and then himself.

Mary sat wordless, barely able to absorb the horror. She felt the pain, deep and intense, for her friend and could only groan, "Oh, no!"

When Job's friends came to comfort him, they hardly recognized him. His body was covered with painful sores, worsened by his scraping with a broken piece of pottery. The friends wept, tore their robes and sprinkled dust on their heads. And they sat with him for seven days and seven nights, unable to speak to him "because they saw how great his suffering was."

Sometimes, when the shared pain is too great for words, the mere presence of a friend gives the unspoken message of support.

Mary could barely speak on learning of her friend's agony; Job's friends sat beside him.

Thank you, Lord, for the strong faith witness of Job in spite of his intense sufferings. Help us to stand by a suffering person, even if we cannot speak.

Have words ever failed you? Did you take any action?

58

■ BRING THE SUNSHINE INSIDE

Psalm 142: "When the spirit grows faint within me, it is you who know the way. . . . no one is concerned for me. . . . no one cares for my life" (vv. 3-4).

You know I prayed this morning that the Lord would send me something or someone to brighten my day, and—" Myrtle paused, looking directly into Sarah's eyes and chuckled, "you are it!"

This old friend from out of town had come to visit Myrtle, who was severely impaired, both in vision and hearing. Ballooning ankles and legs slowed her walk. Few people came to see her. Sarah's brief visit brought Myrtle the warmth of caring, the joy of being remembered, a sense of being valued as a friend.

When our lives are filled with commitments to family, work, church and school interests, it is difficult to imagine anyone lonely. Yet many suffer an aching emptiness and respond warmly to an occasional visit. Physical limitations or fear of crime may literally imprison elderly in their living space. With the gradual loss of friends through death or illness, their contact with the outside world is even more restricted. They may soon feel that no one remembers them.

The smallest gesture, whether a personal note, a brief visit, a potted plant, a single flower, or a phone call may well bring a response which is joyfully spontaneous, deep and lasting.

> Help us to see, Lord, opportunities to bring a bit of joy into lives of lonely people who may feel that no one is concerned for them or cares about their lives.

Bring a ray of sunshine to a lonely person.

■ WHO CARES FOR CAREGIVERS?

Gal. 6:7-10: "Let us not become weary in doing good, for at the proper time we will reap a harvest if we do not give up" (v. 9).

Sometimes—" Alice started, paused, cleared her throat, and hesitated. "Sometimes I wonder if anybody really cares about us."

Her words were painful to hear. Her years as a conscientious, dedicated, hospital staff nurse were exemplary. She was the kind of nurse a nurse would want if she were ill. But she felt unsupported. She was not seeking praise; she was tired. Tired of being called in for extra shifts. Tired of working short-staffed. Tired of having no head nurse to give directions and to coordinate efforts. Tired of being called to stay home on a scheduled day because she was not needed, then only to be called to come in. Yet, she continued to answer the needs of others.

"I guess," she sighed, "what I want to say is: we do what we are asked, and I suppose we will keep on doing so, but, honestly, it would mean so much if someone along the line would just say a simple thank you."

As one nurse asked, "Who cares for caregivers?"

The slower pace of yesteryear seems to be gone forever. Few people are immune to pressures resulting from economic stresses. Yet, midst it all, we should remember to give words of encouragement. Christ asks that we not become weary in doing good.

 Bless, Lord, the caregivers who so faithfully serve you. Grant them strength for their daily tasks and a sense of your blessing.

How do you thank those who serve you?

60

■ WISHING FOR WINGS

Ps. 55:4-8: "My heart is in anguish within me; . . . .
Fear and trembling have beset me; horror has
overwhelmed me. I said, 'Oh, that I had the wings of
a dove! I would fly away' " (vv. 4-6).

David's eloquence throughout the psalms offers
pleadings, praise and joyful expressions which may
often communicate our deepest feelings at various
times in our lives.

Karen, a hospital social worker, deals with victims of
severe emotional, physical and sexual abuse. Although
serving primarily the inner city residents, Karen
insists that the problem crosses all economic groups.

The abuse is so emotionally debilitating that the
victim may choose not to feel, thus dissociating herself
from the pain. The abused person, feeling like a
prisoner of war, is in a situation similar to a
concentration camp. She or he cannot physically flee,
and fears to fight the abuser.

One child, beaten regularly every Saturday morning
by her father, remembered hearing the cheerful birds
singing nearby. "I would imagine myself up in the tree
with the bird," she explained to Karen. It was her
mental escape from the harshness of reality.

Another child, repeatedly abused by her father,
said, "There was a large water spot on the ceiling. In
my mind I went up there until he left."

 Holy Spirit, work through those who touch the
lives of the abused, that your love may be
manifested to your hurting children.

**Memorize Gal. 5:6, "The only thing that counts is
faith expressing itself."**

■ KINDNESS: A GIFT OF THE SPIRIT

Eph. 4:29-32: "Be kind and compassionate to one another, forgiving each other, just as in Christ God forgave you" (v. 32).

Jenny," Anna called to her friend, reaching out to touch her hand as the aide quickly pushed Jenny's wheelchair down the hall. Jenny did not acknowledge Anna's greeting. They were long-standing friends, now in their 90th years.

"Why didn't Jenny speak?" Anna wondered. She felt hurt.

Later, as Anna rested on her bed, aide Patsy touched her lightly on her arm. "Anna," she called. "I'm sorry I couldn't stop for you to talk to Jenny. You see she became very ill in the dining room. She had to lie down right away."

"Oh, I see," Anna sighed. "Thank you, dear. Tell me. How is she now?"

"Well, Anna, she is very weak. She will have to stay in bed."

"Oh," Anna nodded, and fell silent and motionless except for the gentle interweaving of her fingers and faint movement of her lips.

Next morning Anna learned that Jenny was still very ill. Without a word to anyone, Anna tottered down the hall to Jenny's room. Her frail form barely supported the guitar which she held in her right hand.

"I have come to sing for you, Jenny," she called as she entered her room.

Shortly, a medley of folk tunes and hymns wafted into the hallway.

> Help us, Lord, to forgive hurts, and to respond with kindness.

Can you forgive and forget?

■ PEACE: A GIFT OF THE SPIRIT

John 16:29-33: " 'I have told you these things, so
that in me you may have peace' " (v. 33).

You can never work effectively for peace until you
have peace in your own heart. So Tessie Durloch
learned when the world was spending one thousand
times more for armaments than for the then-existing
League of Nations. She pleaded for money for peace,
but a coworker bluntly told her money was not the
answer, God was.

She searched until she found that peace was rooted
in faith in God and love of humanity.

Studies by Harvard Medical School Professor
Herbert Benson demonstrated measurable
physiological benefits from meditative prayers.

Benson's technique was based on 10 to 20 minutes
at a set time twice daily in a relaxed position, eyes
closed, passively meditating on a short scripture
passage or a phrase, i.e. "Jesus is Lord." He suggests
breathing slowly, silently repeating the phrase as you
exhale.

William Proctor writes: "It almost seems that God
has orchestrated *all* reality, so that our bodies as well
as our spirits respond positively as we cultivate a deep
relationship with him."

Lord, help us set aside daily quiet time to
meditate, to sense the peace which you have
promised.

Repeat this blessing today:
May the Lord bless you and keep you. May the Lord
let his countenance shine upon you and be gracious
unto you. May the Lord turn his face toward you and
give you peace.

■ WHO IS JESUS' BROTHER?

Mark 3:31-35: " 'Whoever does God's will is my brother and sister and mother' " (v. 35).

When Jesus asked who his mother and brothers were, he answered his own question. He said that anyone who does what God wants him to do is his brother, sister, and mother.

As a youth I wondered why we had so many church denominations. I later learned to appreciate the richness of diversity. Today I welcome the ecumenical direction in which our churches are moving. It is good to celebrate our oneness in Christ.

While a student nurse in a Lutheran hospital, I was keenly aware of the Catholic hospital next door to ours. It seemed superfluous. Weren't we, I wondered, each extending our Christian ministry to the sick? Couldn't we be doing this together?

Years later I had an opportunity to return to work in a newly opened unit of "my" hospital. One Sunday when I had a chance to attend chapel with several patients, I was deeply touched as I listened to a Catholic nun presenting the familiar story of Jesus calming the storm. I had heard or read the story many times. The telling and the interpretation were not that different, but on that particular day, it was *our* story.

 Thank you, Lord, for our brothers and sisters in faith. Bless the work of all to your honor and glory.

Seek ways to work, study, pray together with others who want to do the will of God.

■ AND ANGELS CAME

Matt. 4:1-11: "Then the devil left him, and angels came and attended him" (v. 11).

It was Karen's second day as float nurse in coronary care. Mr. Schevenko's heart condition had stabilized, but he looked downcast and troubled. His eyes focused on the title of a booklet jutting from Karen's pocket: *Ministry of Angels*, it read.

Karen held the book toward him, "I was reading this on my break. Would you like to look at it?"

"No," he shrugged, falling silent.

"You seem so sad today, Mr. Schevenko. Is there anything I can do for you?"

"No," he sighed. "No, nothing." Then, hesitantly, "I am sad, because I am so alone. Maybe I was wrong when I left my country. In Russia I thought only 'come to America to be free.' Now so many years have passed and I do not know of my children."

Closing his eyes, he clasped his hands together. His voice cracked as he spoke. "It hurts double to know I am here and they are there."

"Maybe," Karen smiled, "angels are watching over your family in Russia."

Before leaving, she prayed softly that he might be released from his sadness and be at peace knowing God was watching over them.

A gentle smile broke his sober countenance. His lips said a silent "thank you."

 Lord, thank you for angels who lighten troubled hearts by pointing them to you.

A reassurance: "For he will command his angels concerning you to guard you in all your ways" (Ps. 91:11).

■ AS THE TWIG IS BENT

Prov. 22:6: "Train up a child in the way he should go, and when he is old he will not turn from it."

The chaplain's benediction over the intercom signaled the closing of the morning service. I was outside Anna's door when I saw her seated, head bowed, hands folded. A pot of yellow chrysanthemums added a burst of beauty to the tranquil scene. Looking up, she called, "Come in. Come in." Then, "Oh, it is so nice, so nice. I sit in my room and I hear. Ya, it is like in the church."

Hearing the worship allowed Anna to continue her lifelong habit of Sunday worship.

Working with elderly has proved a testimonial to our verse; the habit of worship continues whether it is in the chapel, in a room, or in a hallway via intercom.

So, too, we see the faithful in communion. If unable to go to chapel, then in their rooms. It satisfies a hunger for renewal through forgiveness.

When 100-year-old Clara needed assistance in walking to chapel, her major concern was her purse. She must take her offering, she said.

And how often we hear frail elderly praying old familiar words, memorized years ago, or audibly asking the Lord to bless the nurses that day.

In worship, in communion, in giving and in prayer these habits of faith are sustenance in twilight years.

 Thank you, Lord, for homes where elderly may continue to receive spiritual nourishment. Keep us in the teachings of our childhood.

In what way do you support and encourage such homes?

■ BEING STILL BEFORE GOD

Psalm 46: "Be still, and know that I am God; I will be exalted among the nations, I will be exalted in the earth" (v. 10).

Prayer is a force as real as terrestrial gravity. I have seen people, after all other therapy had failed, lifted out of disease and melancholy by serene effort of prayer.

"It is the only power in the world that seems to overcome the so-called 'laws of nature'; the occasions on which prayer supplies them with a steady flow of sustaining power in their lives." These words were spoken by Alexis Carrel, a doctor who lived from 1873 to 1944. Many doctors would agree with his words today.

David said blessed is the man whose "delight is in the law of the Lord, and on his law he meditates day and night. He is like a tree planted by the water, which yields fruit in due season" (Ps. 1:1-3).

We are blessed when we see God in the smile of a child, in the orderliness of the universe, in the miracles of nature.

We are blessed when we take time to be still before God, to be still and learn of God. To meditate upon God's love for us which is manifested in all aspects of our lives. To give thanks for God's many blessings to us. To seek God's guidance in our daily lives.

 Help us, Lord, to be still before you in praise, in thanksgiving, and in seeking your will.

Think of the many blessings you experienced today.

■ A PROMISE FULFILLED

John 5:24-29: ". . . whoever hears my word and believes him who sent me has eternal life" (v. 24).

Because Ellen worked only two days a week at our nursing home, she made a special effort to find time for tasks which would help her learn to know residents better. One day she chose to update Margit's care plan by talking to her about her needs.

Chapel services had been important to Margit, but she no longer attended because she could not hear. Ellen asked, "Would you like to have your hearing tested? A hearing aid might help."

"Oh, no-no-no. I get along all right. The Lord will take me home soon. No-no-no." She sat quietly, hands folded, gently self-assured, accepting.

When she admitted that she could no longer read her beloved Norwegian newspaper, Ellen suggested, "Maybe new glasses would help."

Again, "Oh, no-no-no. I should say not. I know the Lord has promised to take me home." Then, with a twinkle in her eyes, she added, "I know he will. I keep asking him."

Two days later, Margit retired to sleep and did not awaken. She went, as promised, home to her Lord.

How beautiful is the faith of those who trust in God and see God's promises fulfilled in their lives.

 Thank you, Lord, for the opportunity to hear your Word. Thank you for your promise of eternal life for us and for all who believe in you.

How do you reflect your faith in your daily life?

■ WHEN WE CANNOT PRAY

Rom. 8:15-27: "The Spirit helps us in our weakness. We do not know what we ought to pray, but the Spirit intercedes for us with groans that words cannot express" (v. 27).

When I woke up in the hospital, I knew my (suicide) attempt had failed. I couldn't believe I was alive. The doctor said it was a miracle. Suddenly life seemed unbelievably precious. If the Lord spared my life, he must have a purpose."

Ann listened to Joan, stunned. "She is the last person in the world I would have considered a potential suicide victim," she thought.

So it is. Often no clue, no suspicion. Few victims make it to the emergency room. Increasingly, youth are taking their lives. Loved ones, family, and friends grieve deeply and feel helpless. Prayer is difficult. The churnings of their hearts leave them wordless.

But we are promised that in our weakness the Spirit intercedes for us with groans that words cannot express.

A pastor said that the grief he experienced after his son's suicide gave him a new understanding of "He descended into hell," but added, "In the depths of depression I felt nestled in the hands of God. When grief is surrounded and filled with grace, it links us with the eternal."

Thank you, Lord, that when we cannot pray, your Holy Spirit intercedes for us in accordance with God's will.

Be open to listen if opportunities come—to friends, coworkers, youth.

■ STRENGTH FOR THE WEARY

Isa. 40:29-31: "He gives strength to the weary and increases the power of the weak. . . . but those who hope in the Lord will renew their strength. . . . They will run and not get weary, they will walk and not be faint" (vv. 29, 31).

I had worked as a nurse at Washington County General Hospital for 10 years when we had to face the physical move into our new facility," Rita explained. "Our newborn infants were transported from small, crowded quarters to a very spacious area with special intensive care units and many isolation rooms. Although our staff had previewed the new hospital space, we were overwhelmed with the task.

"I valued my nursing experiences at the old hospital and was especially grateful for our dedicated nursing staff. Yet, in spite of careful advance planning and support of good workers, I felt physically and emotionally drained as I faced the move.

"Then, the words of Isaiah gave me great strength and hope. 'He gives strength to the weary and increases power of the weak.' "

"On the day of our move two of our babies were in unstable, very critical condition. They required close supervision and much care.

"Staff members were working double shifts and extra days to provide necessary coverage until new staff could be oriented. Yet the Lord gave us the strength to continue."

 Thank you, Lord, for your promise of strength when our tasks seem overwhelming.

A promise: For those who hope in the Lord, he will renew their strength.

70

■ LAUGHTER ON THE OUTSIDE

Prov. 14:13: "Even in laughter the heart may ache, and joy may end in grief."

Yeah," Jane chuckled, subconsciously stroking her abdomen, "the kids bounce around saying 'no problem' and we walk around with a pain in our gut."

Jane's years of nursing experience well qualified her for her night supervisory position. Her quick wit and hearty laugh eased many tense situations, but a crisis was handled with a no-nonsense approach. Having raised a large family, she had an understanding for her staff and their concerns.

In the quiet of early morning rounds, Jane stopped to see Maggie, the first floor nurse. They talked of Maggie's son. "I don't like what he does and I tell him," said Maggie, "but he just shrugs his shoulders, says, 'No problem, mom,' and bounces out the door. I see him hurting himself and that hurts me."

"You don't have to live a long life to recognize the value of such basic teachings as the Ten Commandments," Jane said. "Honoring God and respecting others makes life good for all, but these kids seem to think we should toss it all out the window."

It *is* painful when values, tested and true, are rejected by those we love. Tossing aside tested values leads to chaos and tension. Our behavior does affect those who love us.

 Tune our hearts, Lord, to recognize laughter which may cover pain.

Listen to laughter with your heart.

■ WORDS OF HOPE

Prov. 15:30: "A cheerful look brings joy to the
heart, and good news gives health to the bones."

Although caregivers, professional or otherwise, have
many occasions to share the pain of others, they also
give good news. From the doctor's office: "The biopsy
was negative." In the delivery room: "It's a healthy
baby boy." Outside the intensive care unit: "Your
father is responding."

The prison chaplain announces: "The parole board
voted unanimously to grant you parole."

The marriage counselor says, "After speaking to you
individually, I see a sincere desire in each of you to
make your marriage work. I would be happy to help
your efforts toward that goal."

Sometimes the news cannot be good. The biopsy
may be positive. The baby may have breathing
problems. Then we bring the news with cheerful
honesty.

"The biopsy is positive, but with a few radiation
treatments, we hope. . . ."

"Your baby has difficulty breathing. We believe this
is temporary."

Good news releases us, relieves our tensions, and
contributes to our good health. Even disheartening
news is accepted with reduced anxiety when we speak
with a cheerful countenance and offer a word of hope.

 Thank you, Lord, for the opportunities to give
good news to others. Help us to bring hope
with a cheerful countenance when the news is
less good.

What is the best news Christ brought to us?

■ ARE WE SOUL-CARERS?

Matt. 9:35-38: "When he saw the crowds, he had compassion on them, because they were harassed and helpless, like sheep without a shepherd" (v. 36).

Much of Jesus' ministry included not only teaching and preaching the news of the kingdom, but also healing. Repeatedly Jesus restored sight to the blind, cured lepers, made the lame walk and the deaf to hear. In today's Bible verse we read that when Jesus saw the crowds, he had compassion on them. Jesus truly was a soul-carer. Jesus expressed his compassion when he looked at the crowds, "harassed and helpless, like a sheep without a shepherd."

Seeing so many people with needs for soul and body, he felt deep concern saying, "The harvest is plentiful, but the workers are few." He then gave his disciples authority to heal every disease and sickness. "Freely you have received," he said, "freely give" (Matt. 10:8).

As caregivers we see grievous needs of soul and body. We see victims of terminal and chronic illness, crippling conditions, physical and mental abuse, and broken spirits. Christ asks us, as his followers, to show compassion to these people in need. We, who have been given much, can give freely in whatever competency we possess. We may give medical advice, perform nursing procedures, support families emotionally, speak comforting words, pray with them, or request chaplaincy visits. Each action, in the name of Christ, is soul-caring.

 Lord, help us show your compassion to others.

For one week explore opportunities to show Christ's caring.

■ TWO PROMISES

Ps. 29:11: "The Lord gives strength to his people; the Lord blesses his people with peace."

Birgit's Swedish ancestry was undeniable. White hair edged her pink-white face. Smile-lines accented her ice blue eyes. But her genteel manner belied an underlying iron will. If the nursing home staff had known about her past promises, they might have been more understanding. Not knowing, they saw Birgit as a problem. She refused to get up in the morning. In spite of many efforts, no approach worked.

One evening, after supper, Birgit sat in the front yard until dusk. She delighted in the fresh air and enjoyed watching the sparrows and the squirrels. At dusk, when she plodded back to her room, Sally, the evening nurse, met her.

Giving her a gentle hug, Sally suggested, "You know, Birgit, if you got up in the morning, you could be out much of the day."

Birgit turned, looked directly into Sally's eyes, and said, "Well, I tell you, when I was a young girl in Sweden, I worked long, hard days. Then when I came to America I worked in a home from early morning till late at night. I just prayed the Lord for strength for each day, and he gave it to me. But I promised *myself*, that when I could sleep in the morning, I would."

 Thank you, Lord, for answered prayers and kept promises.

Can you think of a situation in your life when a simple statement of your faith would have explained your actions?

74

■ WORDS OF HOPE

Hebrews 11: "Now faith is being sure of what we hope for and certain of what we do not see" (v. 1).

Behind the drawn curtain, the pastor stood at the bedside of his parishioner who was gravely ill. He prayed that the Lord would bless the man and grant him peace in his heart. And he gave thanks to the Lord for the Lord's healing power.

In the same hospital, weeks later, a complete stranger called to him, "Hey, Pastor!"

Straining to recognize the face, the pastor hesitated, then said, "I'm sorry. I don't believe I know you."

"I'm Charlie, Pastor," he said, grinning widely. "I had hoped to see you again. I wanted to thank you for saving my life."

"Saving your life?" the pastor asked.

"Yes," Charlie explained, "you see I was in the ward when you visited Hans Gmeiner. I was in a deep coma much of the time, but I heard you praying with Hans. When you thanked the Lord for his healing power, you gave me hope. For the first time, I thought maybe I *could* get well. From then on I fought hard to regain my health. Because of your prayer, I got well."

The sincere prayer of a devout Christian often leads others to a deeper faith and holds before them words of encouragement and strength. What a precious gift to a discouraged soul!

 Grant, Lord, the opportunity and the ability to give words of hope to those who desperately need them.

Do you know someone who needs a word of hope today?

75

■ FAITHFULNESS: GIFT OF THE SPIRIT

Rev. 2:10: "Be faithful, even to the point of death, and I will give you the crown of life."

An employee of 35 years is a rare person. But so is Olga. In 1951 she came to work at a care center after reading about it in a magazine.

"I was impressed with the large, beautiful yard and the homelike atmosphere," she said. "And it was good to see how elderly residents visited with each other in the lounge."

Olga started work as a housekeeper on second floor in April of that year. She was more like a member of the extended family than an employee. She not only was faithful in her work, but genuinely cared for the residents.

In a homelike atmosphere residents became family to each other. But failing health would raise fear in their hearts. They did not fear death; they feared a possible move to another nursing facility if they could not care for themselves.

Keenly aware of this, Olga would quietly work in their behalf to help them remain independent as long as possible when their health failed. She made difficult days easier for them by smoothing their paths.

 Thank you, Lord, for your faithful servants who convey your love to others in their daily work.

In what ways are you faithful at work? with family? with friends? to God?

■ OF WISDOM AND UNDERSTANDING

Job 12:12: "Is not wisdom found among the aged? Does not life bring understanding?"

I should have been born with a classroom seat attached to me, I enjoy the opportunity to learn," my 80-year-old friend said. "Here in the United States the emphasis is on the body. In England they stress exercise of the *mind*."

At a glance she could professionally critique my writing. Years earlier her interest in social issues led her to a full scholarship at the University of Chicago. "I became a grandmother and a college student on the same day," she said.

When asked for advice for people in their eighties, she urged wise choices in activity, food, and thought. "Physical activity is essential. And," she advises, "junk foods and self-pity will not make for health and happiness in your eighth decade of life.

"Reaching out to others brings blessings; self-pity and isolation brings misery. Learn something new each day. Have something to look forward to.

"Above all," she says, "practice the presence of God" through Scripture, quiet, and listening to God's voice. "It helps us cope and gives us a deeper insight into real oneness with Christ."

 Thank you, Lord, for the life wisdom of your saints.

What older person has been a source of understanding for you?

■ DOING GOD'S WILL

Ps. 143:3-10: "Teach me to do your will, for you are my God, may your good spirit lead me on level ground" (v. 10).

I do not understand this," the doctor proclaimed as he dropped the phone onto the nurse's desk. "Ethically, I believe a nurse is just as obligated to respond to calls for patient needs as a doctor is." It was his fourth attempt to find a private duty nurse for a patient in that small community.

The doctor's statement bothered Esther, a nurse from the adjoining room giving individual care to a critically ill patient for the night. Reluctantly she had responded to an earlier call. She had left her young family at home, one child just recovering from a painful ear infection. It seemed unfair for her husband to have to get up at night with a crying child. She felt torn between nursing and family needs.

Esther understood why young mothers could not easily leave their families for these calls to duty. It was a difficult decision. Nurses feel the responsibility of both areas, ill patients and their family needs. In a small community where Esther lived, the dilemma presented itself repeatedly.

"I earnestly seek the Lord's will," she said. "I feel because I have been given the opportunity to become a nurse, I should serve others. Yet, I know our children are with us only a short while and they are my primary responsibility."

 Help us, Lord, to know your will for our lives. May your Holy Spirit lead us in the right way.

Follow what Prov. 3:5 suggests: "Trust the Lord, lean not on your own understanding."

■ WHEN SELF-PRIDE SLIPS

Gal. 6:1-5: "Each one should test his own actions. Then he can take pride in himself without comparing himself to somebody else" (v. 4).

In these verses Paul says everyone slips once in awhile by doing something he should not do. With love, Christian friends should help him to correct his behavior and to get back onto the right path. Paul's attitude is that it could happen to any of us so we are not to be judgmental, but rather help him to regain a good feeling about himself.

As children grow up they need much reassurance along the way to feel good about themselves. If they do wrong, they must know they may be forgiven, but they must also know they are loved.

Estelle, a mental health worker, frequently deals with low self-esteem in patients. "It is difficult to break their cycle of discouragement," she says. They may have acted wrongly in some way and can not accept themselves as worthwhile people. Gentle guidance in confession and forgiveness may be necessary. With help in setting and reaching goals, their self-pride is slowly restored. Their marriage may be strengthened. The meaningfulness of life can be regained, and productivity will be increased.

"You have more faith in me than I did in myself," one patient told Estelle upon discharge.

 Help us look at our own actions, Lord, and take responsibility for them.

Encourage someone knowing that "The tongue that brings healing is a tree of life" (Prov. 15:4).

■ SERVANTHOOD OR SLAVERY

Phil. 2:5-11: "Your attitude should be the same as that of Christ Jesus: Who . . .taking the very nature of a servant . . . .humbled himself and became obedient to death—even death on a cross!" (vv. 5-8).

A servant responds to the needs of others. Christ was described by Peter as "The Christ of God" in Luke 9:20. Yet Christ went to the extreme in servanthood by dying that we might live.

Servanthood is reaching out to a person at his point of need. It is helping that person grow stronger physically, emotionally, and spiritually.

In nursing we may give physical assistance until the patient regains his strength; we may give emotional support to begin the healing of hurts; we may carefully confront detrimental behavior; we may give spiritual encouragement as our patient shows receptivity. We may be the advocate for our patients by putting them in touch with others who may respond more specifically to their needs, whether it is a chaplain, dietician, doctor, or the patient's family.

Servanthood becomes servitude when we allow prolonged dependency by doing something for someone when she can do it for herself, when we allow ourselves to be manipulated, or when our wholeness is reduced by extended efforts for another. Then our effectiveness is lessened.

 Help us, Lord, to be good servants for you, guarding against the destructive servitude role.

Take time to evaluate your role as servant in relation to whomever you care for.

■ PRIVATE PRAYER

Matt. 6:5-8: "When you pray, go into your room, close the door and pray to your Father, who is unseen. Then your Father, who sees what is done in secret, will reward you" (v. 6).

I think the witness of an older person who has suffered much, yet remained rock solid in her Christian faith, bears a powerful testimony," Rose Ann said.

"Thinking of anyone special?" her friend asked.

"Well, yes, in fact I was. Marcella. First, her daughter's suicide, then two years later her son-in-law's tragic accident which left the three grandchildren without parents. She was able to talk about her pain, yet clearly expressed a belief that the Lord would carry her through.

"I stopped to see her after her husband, Tony, died. She told me how distraught she had been at the sight of all the medical equipment supporting Tony's life. When she talked with his doctor, she learned that recovery or improvement was impossible. Then Marcella said, 'Do whatever you think is best, doctor.'

" 'That night I took the Lord literally,' Marcella said. 'I went into my closet and prayed that he would guide the doctor in his decision. Next morning the machines were gone. Max died in peace last night.'

"She was a woman of prayer."

 Thank you, Lord, for the witness of people who turn to you in prayer seeking guidance.

In what decisions have you sought guidance recently?

81

■ OF WISDOM AND WORK

James 1:2-9: "If any of you lacks wisdom, he should ask God, who gives generously to all without finding fault, and it will be given him" (v. 5).

Well, are you ready to unpack your nursing cap and uniforms?" Joyce's husband asked as she dropped her books onto the kitchen table.

"Hah!" Joyce blurted, collapsing onto the nearby chair. "You know when I saw the ad for the refresher course, I could hardly wait to take it, but now—" she sighed, "after all the lectures, films, orientation to the hospital and even floor duty, I am *afraid*! I am not ready for all that responsibility."

The knowledge and technology explosion extends throughout all fields of work. Is there a nurse in any area who feels completely adequate for her daily tasks? Inservice education and nursing workshops address current and recurring issues for study, yet we find it difficult to keep informed.

As Christians, we want to be a "workman who does not need to be ashamed," but to present ourselves "as one approved of God" (2 Tim. 2:15).

When young Solomon was to become king, he felt very inadequate for his task. He asked God for a discerning heart for two reasons: to govern God's people, and to distinguish between right and wrong. God gave it to him and blessed his reign. We are promised wisdom for the asking and are reminded that we should study to be good workmen.

 Grant us wisdom in discerning matters of the heart and mind as we serve the needs of others.

As God's worker, make a special effort to study in an area where you feel inadequate.

■ WORK AS UNTO THE LORD

Col. 3:22-25: "Whatever you do, work at it with all your heart, as working for the Lord, not for men. . . . It is the Lord Christ you are serving" (vv. 23-24).

A personality profile on the president of a Christian college revealed a man who has a clear sense of service to Christ. In the Air Force he learned about organization, delegation of authority and administration. He demonstrates an ability to quietly motivate people. He combines responsible moral conduct with business. He searches for and fills community needs. These qualities have made him an outstanding head of the college.

He explains the school's excellent business programs saying, "I think a young person could easily aspire to a life of service and at the same time want to be in business and be successful." Then, acknowledging that profits are essential for business success, he adds that businesses concerned only with profits—and not service—"are not going to last very long."

Whether we care for business, body, or soul needs of others, we need to remember that it is the Lord we are serving and pray that our work may reflect the spirit of Christ.

 Lord, may we show honesty, integrity, responsibility, and sincerity in whatever we do.

Practice Christ-awareness in your daily tasks today, mentally offering your work efforts to the Lord.

■ THE LORD WATCHES OVER YOU

Psalm 121: "The Lord will keep you from all harm—
he will watch over your life" (v. 7).

Yes, I recall a time when I felt the Lord was surely
watching over the life of a patient. She was such a
pretty young mother-to-be. When I first saw her lying
in the rumpled sea of white sheets, moist dark ringlets
of hair seemed to soften her facial grimacing as she
suffered one severe convulsion after the other. It
happened long ago, but I can see her as if it were
now."

Marian, a nurse with many years of varied
experiences, was sharing the story of a patient she
could not forget.

"Perhaps today modern medicine has an answer to
such an agonizing situation, but at that time we could
only give the mother-to-be limited medication and try
to prevent injury to herself or her unborn child. The
frequency, intensity, and length of her seizures was
frightening to observe and exhausted her energy.

"I wondered how this mother and child could safely
endure this repeated body stress."

After a thoughtful pause, Marian added, "But the
child did live. Through another nurse from that
hospital I later learned that the mother delivered a
healthy baby girl. To me, it seemed a miracle. I am
often reminded of this situation when I read 'I will
keep you from all harm.' "

 For your miraculous protection of unborn
babes and your sustenance of mothers during
difficult pregnancies, we thank you, Lord.

**When has the Lord's protection seemed to supercede
medical treatment?**

■ FROM DEATH UNTO LIFE

John 11:17-27: "Jesus said to her, 'I am the
resurrection and the life, He who believes in me will
live, even though he dies; and whoever lives and
believes in me will never die. Do you believe this?' "
(vv. 25-26).

Because Kaia had worked at the nursing home for
almost ten years, she had grown exceptionally fond of
some of them.

Sigurd was one of those residents. He was a kindly
gentleman with gray white hair which reminded her of
the familiar proverb: "Gray hair is a crown of splendor;
it is attained by a righteous life" (16:31). Though
slightly stooped, he bore his ninety-year-old body with
an air of dignity and delighted others with his sense of
humor. Kaia often saw him reading his Bible.

When a sudden stroke felled him, leaving him
unconscious, his doctor came to examine him. "A
matter of hours," he said, folding his stethoscope.
"Better notify his family."

Kaia came on night duty just after Sigurd's son had
left. She arranged for a dedicated older nurse's aide to
sit with Sigurd until she could be free from her duties.

When she returned to Sigurd, he was restless.

"I held his hand and prayed that the Lord would
give him a sense of his presence and of peace," Kaia
said.

Minutes later, he quieted. Shortly, life slipped away.

"It was a beautiful spiritual experience," Kaia said.
"I felt like singing the doxology."

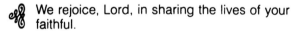 We rejoice, Lord, in sharing the lives of your
faithful.

**Consider this: "Precious in the sight of God is the
death of his saints" (Ps. 116:15).**

■ THE BODY OF CHRIST

1 Cor. 12:12-31: "Now you are the body of Christ, and each of you is a part of it" (v. 27).

Above the altar of our church a gilded outline of the head and shoulders of Christ stands in bold relief on the red-brick chancel wall. At a glance, upon entering, we are reminded that we are parts of the body of Christ. Each of us, as a member of Christ's body, has his own gift or ability to help carry out Christ's work here on earth. And, as each part of the body must serve its function, so must all parts work together.

In an emergency room the doctors, nurses, laboratory technicians and assistants work together as a finely tuned machine to maximize life-saving efforts on behalf of the patient. We may use our individual skill fully in intensive care, newborn nursery, psychiatry, hospice or in our day to day contacts. We may be a caring listener for a burdened soul, a touch of warmth to a love-starved person. Whether we work in the hospital or out, we work toward the benefit of another.

As fellow members of the body of Christ, we function together to carry out Christ's mission. When we are instrumental in relieving pain, easing suffering, bolstering downcast spirits or allaying fears, we are being the hands and heart of Christ.

 Help me, Lord, to use my special gift in carrying out your work.

By sincere praise, encourage a weaker member of the body of Christ. Uphold efforts of coworkers to develop their lesser abilities.

86

■ FAITH IN THE UNSEEN

1 Peter 1:1-9: "Though you have not seen him, you love him; . . .you believe in him and are filled with an inexpressible and glorious joy" (v. 8).

Legally blind? Anna? I knew she was visually handicapped, but blind? I see her walking briskly along the halls without hesitation and she is always so cheerful."

Ruth, a new nurse in the board and care facility, was actively learning more about the residents each day. When another nurse referred to Anna's blindness, Ruth decided to spend time with her resident.

"How did you lose your sight, Anna?" she asked.

"It was quite gradual, really. Actually I had fallen, face-first onto loose gravel causing many facial cuts." It was two years later, Anna said, that a detached retina, beyond restorative repair, was discovered. Within a year she lost sight in the other eye.

"It must have been a very difficult time for you, Anna."

"Yes, it was, but I made up my mind long ago not to complain. I would do what I could and not fuss about what I could not do. But, after all, it is what is *inside* that makes the difference. I know I am in the Lord's hands, so I do not worry."

 Though we do not see you, Lord, we have a sense of joy because our faith is rooted in you.

Do you know someone who is joyous in spite of a handicap?

■ IS EVERYTHING COMING UNGLUED?

Ps. 35:17-28: "O Lord, you have seen this; be not silent. Do not be far from me, O Lord" (v. 22).

In the vernacular telling of this psalm we would say that David has really "had it." In a sense he is saying, "Look, Lord, these people are driving me crazy. Do something. Go after them. Get even! They want to kill me. When I am good to them, they are evil to me. When I stumble, they laugh. They slander and mock me and falsely accuse me. Listen, Lord, you have seen this. *Do something.* Stay close to me. I need you."

Have you ever felt that everything was coming apart for you and your prayers were not answered? David's feelings are pretty strong and he verbalizes them freely. A mental health worker might say it was good he could express his thoughts and feelings when he was so troubled.

Each of us may at some time identify with David's pleadings. We may feel totally powerless. Perhaps someone authoritively questioned our professional judgment and gave us no opportunity for explanation. Perhaps a new job description or procedure which directly affected our daily work was inaccurate, but we were not given an occasion to contribute our input. Like David, we may look to the Lord for help. In Ps. 31:14, David says, "But I trust in you, O Lord, I say 'You are my God.' My times are in your hands." Again in Ps. 52:8 he reaffirms his trust: "But I am like an olive tree flourishing in the house of God; I trust in God's unfailing love for ever and ever."

Thank you, Lord, that you are never far from us, even in our most troubled times.

What do you do when you feel that everything is coming unglued?

■ OUR BODIES A TEMPLE

1 Cor. 6:19-20: "Do you not know that your body is the temple of the Holy Spirit. . . . You are not your own" (v. 19).

Paul pleads for moral purity. He reminds us through his writing that our bodies are the temple of the Holy Spirit. Our bodies are not our own to do with as we please.

What do we know about the Holy Spirit within us? According to Jewish thought, the Holy Spirit was the person who brought God's truth to them. According to Paul, a person could say "Jesus is Lord" only when the Spirit enabled him to say it. Martin Luther explains that the Holy Spirit calls, gathers, enlightens, sanctifies, and keeps us in the truth. Surely, if our bodies are the temple of the Holy Spirit, we should strive for maximum wellness.

Today, holistic health addresses not only the physical, but also the psychological, and spiritual aspects. We are in a wellness trend with exercise and fitness classes, health food stores, and a flood of nutritional information. Support groups abound for psychological problems. Spiritual counseling is often available.

We try to keep elderly persons functioning at home with help, thus allowing the I-can-do-it attitude to supercede the expectation of care. Instead of a focus on *recovery from* illness, we aim for *prevention*.

As temples of the Holy Spirit, we are not our own. We belong to God.

 Help us, Lord, to keep our bodies worthy temples thus honoring Thee.

Examine yourself, holistically, as a temple of the Holy Spirit.

■ UNTO THE LEAST OF THESE

Matt. 25:31-40: "Whatever you did for the least of these brothers of mine, you did it for me" (v. 40).

Police found him lying on the street, inebriated. He has a fracture, left tibia."

Surely, I thought, *they wouldn't assign this man to one of us.* We were fledgling probationers on our first eight-hour day of floor duty standing at starched-white attention for the night nurse's report.

She continued, but my mind kept returning to the man in room 105.

As patients were assigned, my greatest fear was confirmed. "Miss Groth: 105. Complete bedbath. Good cast care and observation."

Later, during the extensive mouth care and many-basin bath I talked to the man. Then, swallowing frequently to keep the lump down in my throat, I pulled the washcloth between each of his swelling toes. Twice his eyes seemed to follow me.

I thought of home and questioned my choice of profession. After a thorough backrub, linen change and careful positioning, I tucked the signal cord into his open hand. Tears welled in his eyes. His lips moved, but no words came.

Unknown, the chart read under "whom to notify." As I wondered if anyone cared, I remembered Christ's words, "Whatsoever you did for the least of these, *brothers of mine,* you did it for me."

 Help us always, Lord, to see the hungry, the sick, the imprisoned and the stranger in need as our brother.

Consider our unique opportunities to serve "the least of these."

◼ FOOLS FOR CHRIST

1 Cor. 4:9-16: "We are fools for Christ. . . . I urge you to imitate me" (vv. 10, 16).

Paul wrote to the Corinthians that he felt he was "made a spectacle to the whole universe" because of the way he and other Christians lived. "When we are cursed, we bless. When we are persecuted, we endure it; when we are slandered, we answer kindly."

During the rebellious Vietnam years, young men commonly wore their hair long. In their antiestablishment protest, they often turned away from church attendance. At that time a young soft-spoken psychiatric assistant with gently waved shoulder length hair was overheard in discussion with his coworkers: "I can eliminate the normal church worship from my life, but I can not ignore the life of Christ."

What an impact the life of Christ had on this young man! What was Christ's life like? Christ said we should turn the other cheek, go the extra mile, love our enemies and pray for those who persecute us. We should give to the needy, visit the sick, and the imprisoned, and be kind to strangers. He healed the blind, the sick, the dumb. He was a friend to tax collectors and sinners. He spent his life for others. "The Son of Man did not come to be served, but to serve" (Matt. 20:28).

 Help us, Lord, to be fools for you in serving others.

Think of times you have been a fool for Christ. What did you do? How did you feel?

91

■ PATIENCE: A GIFT OF THE SPIRIT

Rom. 15:1-7: "May the God who gives endurance
and encouragement give you a spirit of unity among
yourselves as you follow Christ Jesus" (v. 5).

Does anything remain the same? Changes occur at a
rapid pace in most work areas. Modern technology.
Computers. The medical field is not an exception. Do
you ever feel that if there is *one* more change you may
quit the job?

With increasing medicare forms, and escalating
malpractice insurance rates doctors surrender to
increasing pressures. They become discouraged and
may even feel like giving up.

In our reading today, Paul encourages his brothers
in Christ to endure in spite of discouragement. He
urges the strong to assist the weak, to build him up for
his good.

He adds in verses 5-7: "May the God who gives
endurance and encouragement give you a spirit of
unity among yourselves as you follow Christ Jesus, so
that with one heart and mouth you may glorify the
God and Father of our Lord Jesus Christ."

"Accept one another then, just as Christ accepted
you, in order to bring praise to God."

Jesus repeatedly tells us to ask for our needs,
believing, in prayer, and he will give them. He will
give us patience to endure and will encourage our
efforts.

 Dear God, give us the patience to encourage
others and to work together to glorify you.

**Remember to accept one another, just as Christ
accepted you.**

■ FAITHFULNESS CROWNED

Rev. 2:10: "Be faithful, even to the point of death, and I will give you a crown of life."

When my father managed a county farm, mother served as home manager for in-house residents, besides caring for our family. Each afternoon, after a short nap, she sat in her small rocking chair, Bible on her lap, reading. This held top priority.

Widowed at age 52, she was left with few possessions, but a strong faith. From that time on, she was constantly helping others. First, home care for the elderly, then assisting each of her sisters during prolonged illnesses. In spite of her rootlessness, she never showed or expressed fear of her future.

Though she lost her sight and her general health waned, a touch of humor bubbled through her conversations. She radiated a sense of peace.

As her heart failed, so did her mental acuities. Her consciousness seemed to fade away for brief periods.

One evening, I sat at her bedside awaiting a lucid moment. Finally, she spoke slowly. Her words bore an ethereal quality, as from afar, "Now—I am coming—into the presence—of the Lord." I felt like Moses at the burning bush when God said, "You are standing on holy ground."

 Thank you, Lord, for the witness of your faithful servants, and for the promise of eternal life.

Memorize Rev. 2:10, "Be faithful, even to the point of death, and I will give you a crown of life."

■ SIGHT AFTER BLINDNESS

John 9:13-34: "One thing I do know. I was blind but now I see" (v. 25).

Imagine the joy of a man, blind since birth, receiving his sight! Today surgical miracles restore sight; specific medications delay visual loss. The restoration of sight makes all things new; the delay of threatened loss makes each day's vision priceless. When we have been given the precious gift of sight, we can so easily take it for granted.

How often do we see, but not see at all? We sleepwalk through awesome scenes and wonders of the moment. Too frequently we are jarred by a narrow escape in life, a frightening diagnosis or loss of a loved one before we stop to truly *see* the beauty in everyday living.

Picture yourself watching colored slides projected before you in a dimly lit room. Mentally, with eyes closed, look at each one carefully. Immerse yourself in the beauty of the scene: A patch of crocuses bursting through lightly crusted snow; splashes of gold, bronze, scarlet, orange, green, and yellow leaves illuminating hills and valleys, streets and roadsides; ducks, silhouetted against rippled golden waters at sundown; rhythmic splashes of white-tipped surf against time-smoothed rock and gnarled trees; sprays of fireworks exploding radiance into a black velvet sky; the serenity of a smile wrinkled face bent over tissue thin covered hands folded in prayer.

 For the magnificence of your world, the precious gift of life, and the miracle of sight to enjoy them all, we thank you, Lord.

Daily look anew at the world today for the beauty of each moment.

■ SEARCH AND KNOW

Ps. 139:23-24: "Search me, O God, and know my heart; . . .See if there is any offensive way in me" (vv. 23-24).

A classmate, JoAnn, told of a Christmas Eve when she worked on a surgical floor. In retrospect, she smilingly says, "To be honest, I was not there because I wanted to be there, not on Christmas Eve!" She had been married only six months. She could not be with her husband during his basic army training, and because of her work, could not even be with her own family. She was feeling sorry for herself when she answered Mr. Rutsa's light.

Beads of perspiration dotted his ruddy face. "I don't think this is working," he said, glancing toward the bottles connected to his gastric suction tube. His abdomen was distended; the tubing plugged.

JoAnn started to irrigate slowly. After repeated flushes, the tubing finally drained freely; the painful pressure was relieved. As she turned to leave, Mr. Rutsa thanked her, adding, "Your mother must be very proud of you."

She stopped, winced, muttered something like "Thank you" and hurried into the hallway.

"*Would* my mother be proud of me if she knew my selfish thoughts?" she wondered. "More than anything else I wanted to be with family tonight."

 Search our hearts, Lord. Help us to see what is offensive to you. Grant us a spirit of joy in service for you.

Memorize Ps. 100:2, "Serve the Lord with gladness."

■ CHRIST—LIGHT AND LIFE

John 1:1-13: "In him was life, and that life was the light of men" (v. 4).

Because nurses see people of all ages in the balance between life and death, we value life. Yet, with modern methods and machines, we also see the prolongation of life beyond what seems reasonable. Hospital policy requires cardiopulmonary resuscitation unless otherwise ordered by the doctor, usually in agreement with patient and family. We have seen vegetable existences and devastating hospitalization costs following rescue attempts through CPR, but for many it means a new chance at life.

An inveterate alcoholic, suffering from a deteriorating physical condition which included severe liver damage was precariously near death. Staff nurses wondered if intravenous feedings should be continued. Suddenly his heart stopped. CPR was initiated. He lived another week. Was it worth it, one might ask, to resuscitate him only to live one week?

To answer that we would have to look at his week. During that time he came to faith in Christ and a healing of great family pain was begun. Can we question the value of his return to life?

In Christ is life, and that life is the light of men. Christ sheds light into the hearts of men. Through him is forgiveness, love, healing, and hope.

 Help us, Lord, that our actions may help, not hinder, the execution of your will in the lives of those we care for.

Memorize John 1:12, "Yet to those who received him, to those who believed in his name, he gave the right to become the children of God."

■ HOW TO LOVE YOUR NEIGHBOR

James 2:8-12: "If you really keep the royal law found in Scripture, 'Love your neighbor as yourself,' you are doing right. But if you show favoritism, you sin" (vv. 8-9).

Dr. Hafdan Mahlur, World Health organization director, reported that highly developed countries of the world, roughly 5-10% of the world's population, use 80-90% of the world's health budget.

How do you feel when you read of a child with respiratory problems who has spent his first three and a half years in a hospital intensive care unit? This child is absolutely priceless. But an awareness of the world imbalance in health care forces us to ask how we can best show love to our neighbor as ourself.

In Boston, Mass., parents of a three-month-old boy threatened to file suit against the hospital if more surgery was ordered for their son. After 13 surgical procedures at the cost of a million dollars, the child lives with multiple physical problems. He has decreased brain capacity. His parents begged the hospital to allow him to die in peace, to be free from pain.

Questions of ethics plague doctors and nurses. Does the modern technology of highly developed countries show favoritism? Are we truly loving our neighbors, worldwide, when many lack basic medical care?

 Dear Lord, you know we are between a rock and a hard place in these decisions. Help us to know your will.

Seek ways to show love to our neighbors through teaching, advocacy, education, economic avenues, and motivation of people to genuine concern to those in need.

■ BY THE TOUCH OF A HAND

Matt. 8:1-4: "Jesus reached out his hand and touched the man, ... 'Be clean!' Immediately he was cured of his leprosy" (v. 3).

Sister Rosalind, a petite nun with gentle manner, quoted this verse to the assembled councilmen. She was pleading her case for a reduced licensing fee for her massage business. "I really believe the Lord has called me to do this, and I feel very fulfilled. My whole aim is to bring therapeutic massage into high standards."

"People are literally skin-hungry," she added, "and want to be touched in a healing way. Sometimes they come in for a physical healing. Sometimes for an emotional healing. Sometimes just for a touch."

We are surrounded by brokenness today. Family divisions and household moves shatter family ties with loved ones. Loneliness causes great emptiness. Dr. James J. Lynch in his book, *The Broken Heart*, presents study reports which reveal the medical consequences of loneliness. One study indicates that the warmth of human touch reduces the heart rate even when the patient is otherwise unresponsive.

Workshops on the psychological aspects of aging frequently focus on the importance of touch to the elderly patient. The luxurious twice-a-day backrubs of yesterday were, in fact, therapeutic, relaxing, restorative.

 Lord, through you, may our touch bring warmth to those who feel cold, kindness to those who are in pain, and your love to the lonely.

Increase your awareness, of skin-hungry people who yearn for the warmth of human touch.

■ SERVICE TO GOD

John 12:20-26: "My father will honor the one who serves me" (v. 26).

As I look back over my life I can see how the Lord has led me," said Esther, a 76-year-old retired nurse. She was the youngest of 12 children. "Mother was often ill, so I did housework besides farm duties. Then, when father was critically injured, he depended on me to do the daily farm chores and field work."

She could not attend high school, but took some correspondence courses. At 29 years of age, she started her nursing studies.

During training, when asked to write "Why I Like to Be a Nurse," she wrote: "Where is there a greater need than among the sick? They need to be served, and they do need a friend who is a real friend to them. In serving others, we serve God and we also do his will."

Esther served through the last years of World War II, the devastating polio epidemic, and years of private duty. Physicians sought her services for their patients. After nearly 40 years of nursing, she retired.

"Sometimes I wondered who would care for *me*," she said, "but through all these years I see the hand of God. Now I am able to live independently in a condominium where I have security, the option of meals served, easy access to health care, and opportunities to socialize. The Lord has been good to me."

 Thank you, Lord, for directing our lives when we seek to do your will.

Memorize Psalm 98:1, "Sing to the Lord a new song, for he has done marvelous things."

■ REJOICE ALWAYS

Phil. 4:4-7: "Rejoice in the Lord always. I will say it again: Rejoice!" (v. 4).

Dorothy and Agnes, both physically limited, served as genuine inspirations to others. After her stroke Dorothy admits that she became deeply discouraged. Coming home to three young sons, she was determined to overcome her physical and speech handicaps, but her struggles intensified. One day, on the verge of suicide, she heard her young son cry. "I knew I must go on for him," she said. "*Then* I came to the realization—God was with me. I knew in that moment God still had a purpose in my life."

After rehabilitation, but still striving to speak and walk, Dorothy started volunteering at a local hospital. She realized it is not what a person loses, but what a person can accomplish with what they have left that counts. With a renewed sense of joy, she has spent thousands of hours encouraging those who share her affliction.

Agnes, the other person of inspiration, had good health for many years. Then diabetic complications required the amputation of first one leg, then the other. The visiting nurse, who monitored her condition and her colostomy later, said, "I will always remember her radiant spirit through it all. She would literally lift herself up in the wheelchair and call out, 'Rejoice in the Lord always, and again I say rejoice!' "

 When we feel that we are less than whole in body or spirit, help us, Lord, to see the strengths we do have.

Take time to honestly count your blessings.

■ THE COMFORT OF YOUR PRESENCE

Isa. 43:1-7: "When you pass through the waters, I will be with you" (v. 2).

There is not much I can do except be here," the pastor said after receiving an expression of gratitude for his presence.

Not much? His very "being there" sustained the young couple to whose home he had been called. Minutes earlier, they found their infant son dead in his crib. After leading them in prayer, commending them to the Lord's loving care, their pastor felt helpless. He could not restore life to their precious child. But his presence was of great comfort.

In any loss when the shock and disbelief numbs awareness, when guilt feelings begin to rise and need dispelling, when the wound is fresh and deep, and the tears begin to flow—it is then the visible presence of someone who cares is a source of solace to those who grieve.

Isaiah spoke the Lord's words of comfort to the Israelites in their turmoil when he said, "Fear not. . . . When you pass through the waters I will be with you."

Christ's own parting words to his disciples reassured them: "And surely I will be with you always, to the very end of the age" (Matt. 28:20).

The Lord's words to the Israelites and Christ's departing words to his disciples are words of support which we can share with those who mourn.

 We thank you, Lord, that you are always with us especially in troubled times.

Seek to be a visible presence, a comfort for those who mourn.

101

■ LOVE: FRUIT OF THE SPIRIT

Rom. 12:9-16: "Be devoted to one another in brotherly love. Honor one another above yourselves" (v. 10).

A doctor retired after 58 years of medical practice in a small western town. Not unlike the frontier doctors, he knew the importance of treating the whole person.

"Fifty percent of the people who came to me came because they were troubled. They wanted me to touch their hand, make them feel important. That was something I didn't know when I graduated from medical school."

He listened to patients tell of financial troubles, scolded someone for "tearing around town," or let them cry a little. "Men cry, too. I let him talk, leave him alone for him to dry his eyes and then come back and talk to him some more."

One of his greatest concerns, upon retirement, was who would care for his older patients. His regard was not for himself, but for those he had so faithfully served.

We, in the helping professions, have a unique opportunity to serve others with love. God's love is revealed through us when we show compassionate concern for the welfare and happiness of others.

 Make our lives channels for your love, Lord.

Consider 1 Peter 3:8, "Live in harmony with one another; be sympathetic, love as brothers, be compassionate and humble."

■ ALL THAT IS NEEDED

Rom. 10:5-13: "That if you confess with your mouth
'Jesus is Lord,' and believe in your heart that God
raised him from the dead, you will be saved" (v. 9).

Expired?" The word exploded, involuntarily, from
Martha's lips in reaction to her daughter, Susie's,
message.

"Mercy Hospital called," Susie said. "Aunt Julia
expired at 6:15."

Martha felt a flood of instant guilt. "Died? Alone? I
should have been there." Aunt Julia always seemed to
rebound before. To die, alone! What had happened?

Suddenly, noticing her eight-year-old daughter's
solemn face, Martha said, "Oh, Susie, I'm sorry. Do
you know what that message meant? Aunt Julia died.
She was always good to us. I feel sad that she was
alone."

Feeling helpless, Martha called a friend who worked
at Mercy. Would she know more about Aunt Julia's
death? "No," she said, "but I might be able to find out
for you."

An hour later her call came. "I talked to the nurse
who was with Julia. She said while she was removing
Julia's dinner tray, Julia asked for a Bible. The nurse
found a New Testament. She placed it in Julia's hands
saying that was all she could find.

"Julia said, 'Oh, thank you. That's all I need. That's
all I need.' Those were her last words." Martha knew
what Julia meant. Christ died for her. Because God
raised him up, she also would live again.

 Thank you, Lord, for the confessed faith, of
those who have gone before us.

Whom have you regarded as saints in the faith?

■ WHAT CAN WE GIVE?

1 Peter 4:8-11: "Above all, love each other deeply.
. . . Each one should use whatever gift he has
received to serve others" (vv. 8, 10).

Before Christmas, the president of the Minnesota
Coalition for Terminal Care, wrote a list of gift
suggestions. "When you give one of these gifts, you
give the most priceless gift of all—yourself." (1)
Listening. Psychologists say one of the greatest things
we can do for another is to listen. No interrupting. No
walking away. Just listen. (2) Affection. A Hug, a kiss,
a squeeze of the hand. Tiny actions demonstrate the
great love inside you. (3) A note. To your loved ones.
A simple "I love you" or a sonnet, maybe tucked
somewhere to surprise the receiver. (4) Laughter. Clip
a cartoon, share a riddle, joke or clever article. (5) A
game. Someone else's favorite. Even if you lose, you
shared an experience. (6) A favor. This gift is made
more valuable when it anticipates a request rather
than when it responds to one. (7) A cheerful
disposition. No complaining, self-pity, nasty
comments, pessimistic predictions. (8) Being left
alone. Be sensitive to this need in other's lives. Allow
the gift of solitude, privacy. (9) A compliment. Simple
and sincere: "You look good in blue" or "Good supper,
honey," can be of inestimable value to someone who
feels taken for granted. (10) Prayer. One of the most
valuable gifts we can give. Another way of saying,
"You are so special to me that I often talk to God
about you."

 Lord, help us see opportunities to give the gift
of ourself.

**Review this list occasionally as a reminder for service
to others.**

■ WHEN SOMEONE ELSE CARES FOR YOU

John 21:15-19:   " 'I tell you the truth, when you were younger you dressed yourself and went where you wanted, but when you are old you will stretch out your hands, and someone else will dress you and lead you where you do not want to go' " (v. 18).

Although these words of Jesus to Peter held a very different meaning, they hold much truth regarding elderly people. If, as they age, they lose ability to care for their physical needs, they must rely on others, and they may not always choose to do what is requested of them.

Some of the most dedicated workers in hospitals and nursing homes are the nursing assistants. The value of a good nurse's aide is reflected in all-around good hospital care. A good aide can be depended on to answer lights, to record data, and to report condition changes, freeing the nurse for medication administration, paper and supervisory work.

The aide gives "the cup of cold water" to the patient with fluid loss, perhaps making the difference between early recovery and prolonged illness.

A reliable aide is an absolute blessing if the aide is able to remain patient in spite of an elderly person's slow movement, repetitious phrases, difficulties in speech and independence in thought and behavior. Though the aide may love older people, great patience is required.

 Reward, Lord, your faithful workers whose work honors you.

Be generous in expressing appreciation to faithful assistants.

■ THE LORD GOES BEFORE YOU

Deut. 31:1-8: "The Lord himself goes before you and will be with you; he will never leave you nor forsake you. Do not be afraid; do not be discouraged" (v. 8).

This verse has been very helpful to me many times when I get assigned to different floors, face repeated policy changes, or when I return to work after several days off," a nurse said. "I memorized it years ago and I still feel the tensions leave when I recall it. It comforts me to recall Moses's words to Joshua, 'The Lord himself goes before you and will be with you.' "

Who could better understand God's leading than Moses? During his pilgrimage to the promised land, Moses met many problems. When they needed water, he produced it from a rock. When they needed food, the Lord sent a flock of quails and daily manna. When they encountered bitter water, Moses made it sweet by a miracle. When they had to cross the Red Sea, the Lord parted the waters until the Israelites were safely across. Moses knew the Lord had gone before him. God had not forsaken him through all of these trials.

Do you face an unpleasant task? Do you feel inadequate or discouraged?

 It is comforting to know that you are with us, Lord, and will not forsake us no matter what the trial may be.

When have you felt the Lord has been with you during a difficult time?

■ SUFFICIENT GRACE

2 Cor. 12:7-10: "But he said to me, 'My grace is sufficient for you, for my power is made perfect in weakness' " (v. 9).

Saul, who ruthlessly persecuted Christians, became Paul after his conversion to Christianity. The Lord said, "This man is my chosen instrument to carry my name before the Gentiles and their kings before the people of Israel. I will show him how much he must suffer in my name" (Acts 9:15).

Paul did suffer. He was beaten, imprisoned, and exposed to dangers. He was hungry, thirsty, and cold. In verse seven, he tells of "the thorn in my flesh, a messenger of Satan, sent to torment me."

Scholars do not agree on what the thorn in the flesh was, but it must have been very troublesome. When Paul pleaded three times to the Lord to remove it, the Lord said, "My grace is sufficient for you, my power is made perfect in weakness." Later Paul acknowledges that when he is weak, then he is strong. He turned to the Lord for strength.

How often we see elderly persons coping with weakening heart problems, crippling arthritis, or activity-limiting respiratory distress. Spiritually nourished through chapel services, the reading of God's Word, and private prayer, they learned that the Lord's grace is sufficient for them.

 Thank you, Lord, that your grace is sufficient for us—in every circumstance.

Grace is defined as unmerited favor, mercy, compassion. What has this meant in your life?

■ A BENEDICTION

Heb. 13:20-24: "May the God of peace, . . . equip
you with everything good for doing his will, and may
he work in us what is pleasing to him, through Jesus
Christ, to whom be glory for ever and ever. Amen"
(vv. 20-21).

Whether a caregiver in professional service or a lay
person who is concerned for others, may you be
blessed by these words. May God, the giver of peace,
sustain you in whatever you do and wherever you go.

Let us daily seek the Lord's guidance that we may
do his will, and that our work may be pleasing to him.
In so doing our lives may reflect the thoughts of
George Eliot's poem, *Contagious Heritage.*

> Every soul that touches yours—
> Be it the slightest contact—
> Gets therefrom some good;
> Some little grace; one kindly thought;
> One inspiration yet unfelt,
> One bit of courage
> For the darkening sky,
> One gleam of faith
> To brave the thickening ills of life;
> One glimpse of bright skies
> Beyond the gathering mists—
> To make this life worthwhile
> And heaven a surer heritage.

 Show us your will, Lord, each day that our lives
may reflect your peace.

**Memorize the prayer of St. Francis which opens this
book, "Lord, make me an instrument of thy peace."**

BIBLE READINGS SERIES

Bible Readings for Women
Lyn Klug
Bible Readings for Men
Steve Swanson
Bible Readings for Parents
Ron and Lyn Klug
Bible Readings for Couples
Margaret and Erling Wold
Bible Readings for Singles
Ruth Stenerson
Bible Readings for Families
Mildred and Luverne Tengbom
Bible Readings for Teenagers
Charles S. Mueller
Bible Readings for Mothers
Mildred Tengbom
Bible Readings for Teachers
Ruth Stenerson
Bible Readings for Students
Ruth Stenerson
Bible Readings for the Retired
Leslie F. Brandt
Bible Readings for Church Workers
Harry N. Huxhold
Bible Readings for Office Workers
Lou Ann Good
Bible Readings for Growing Christians
Kevin E. Ruffcorn
Bible Readings for Caregivers
Betty Groth Syverson
Bible Readings for Troubled Times
Leslie F. Brandt
Bible Readings for Farm Living
Frederick Baltz
Bible Readings on Prayer
Ron Klug
Bible Readings on Hope
Roger C. Palms
Bible Readings on God's Creation
Denise J. Williamson

CPSIA information can be obtained at www.ICGtesting.com
Printed in the USA
LVOW12s0010170114

369570LV00001BA/1/P

ABOUT THE AUTHOR

Betty Groth Syverson is a registered nurse and works in the Home Health Department of Parkview Hospital in El Reno, Oklahoma. She brings special Christian care to her nursing service now and has had experience in surgical, psychiatric, and pediatric hospital departments. Betty is a devoted Bible student and active church worker, and has published numerous articles in Christian magazines. She and her husband Lowell have four children.